Daddy, Tell Me A Story

ROBERT YOUNG

Copyright © 2021 by Robert Young.
ryoung2000@hotmail.com
First published in paperback 2010
Second edition 2012
Third edition 2021

ISBN   Softcover   978-1-953537-65-2

All Bible quotes are from the King James Bible unless otherwise stated Scriptures marked KJV are taken from the KING JAMES VERSION (KJV): KING JAMES VERSION, public domain.

Scriptures marked GNB are taken from the GOOD NEWS BIBLE (GNB): Scriptures taken from the Good News Bible © 1994 published by the Bible Societies/HarperCollins Publishers Ltd UK, Good News Bible© American Bible Society 1966, 1971, 1976, 1992. Used with permission.

Scriptures marked NKJV are taken from the NEW KING JAMES VERSION (NKJV): Scripture taken from the NEW KING JAMES VERSION®. Copyright© 1982 by Thomas Nelson, Inc. Used by permission. All rights reserved.

I have avoided mentioning full names of people involved in my stories except for some well-known names.

All rights reserved. No part of this book may be reproduced or transmitted in any form or by any means, electronic or mechanical, including photocopying, recording, or by any information storage and retrieval system without express written permission from the author, except in the case of brief quotations embodied in critical reviews and certain other non-commercial uses permitted by copyright law.

Printed in the United States of America.

To order additional copies of this book, contact:
Bookwhip
1-855-339-3589
www.bookwhip.com

DEDICATION

*This book is dedicated to our Lord Jesus
and to my dear talented children:
Johanna, Jessica and Ruben.*

CONTENTS

Foreword 1
Why I Wrote this Book 3
I Commit My Life to Jesus At 11 Years of Age 4
Man Healed of Tinnitus 6
Healed as a Child 7
Healing of My Big Toe 9
Provided with Work 10
Getting Work in the Fachhochschule 11
My First Bible 12
Laughed at in School 14
My Aggression Removed 16
Baptised at 15 and Preaching in Church at 16 17
The Christian Youth Club 19
A Coffee Table Appears 21
How I Became a Software Engineer 22
Free Physics Tuition 24
I Get a Car for Christmas 25
The 21st Food Packet 27
Can't Live Without You Jesus 28
Opposition from a Project Leader 30
It's Raining Money 32
Blessed with Clothes 34
A Hitchhiker Saves My Day 35
I Win an Oven 37
Johanna is Born 38
I Overcome my Fear of Water Etc. 40
My Right Knee Gets Healed 41

I Give My Car Away	42
"Take One Step Back!"	43
I Write my First Book "Jesus Behind Bars"	44
I Start Working in the Jesus-Group Prison Ministry	46
Jesus is Waiting	47
Prisoners Get Saved!	48
Prisoners Delivered From Nicotine	49
Prisoners Become Preachers	50
Rainbows – A New Job and a New Church	51
My House Gets Broken Into	53
Food Provided	54
Various Prophecies	55
The Lord Gives Me My Desires	57
Side Healed After Fall	58
Four Women Try to Get Me the Sack	59
Susanne's Healings	60
The First Time I Heard God's Voice	61
Terror Act Stopped in Germany	62
God Prepares Me for Church Translation Work	63
The Oldest Woman in Baden Wuerttemberg	64
A Taste of Heaven	66
Help in Trouble	67
Resisting the Devil	68
Healed of a Mysterious Fever	69
Protection Before Birth	70
Saved From an Unseen Death Threat	72
Healed of Sciatica	73
Jesus Provides Me with a Car	74
Healed of Diabetes	75
The "Just in Time" Job	78

The Job Without an Interview	79
A Lump Disappears	81
He Gives us the Desires of our Hearts	82
Fired but then Hired	83
Jesus Pays My Taxes	84
My Guitar Protected From Damage	85
Wonders at Work	86
It Just Keeps on Printing	87
A Girl Decides Against Abortion	89
It's Time for Africa	91
One Star Hotel Christmas Musical	92
Food Bill Paid	94
"Something Great Will Happen"	95
Healed of Bell's Palsy	96
Finger Healed Before the Prayer	98
A Prophecy Comes True	99
The Matecat Miracle	101
Working as a Translator	102
Pension Higher Than Expected	103
200 CHF Returned After Giving Someone Money	104
2 Girls Found After Disappearing While Going to School	105
My Trip to the Ukraine War Zone	106
My Trip to North Korea 2015 - Seeing Angels	109
Get a CS Job Due to Prophecy	112
The Broken Finger	114
Translation of a Children's Book in 2 Weeks	115
Healings Using Emails, Texts or Social Media	116
I Get a Room for Free	118
The Miracle Man Musical	119
A Woman's Face Cancer Healed	120

41-Day Fast	122
1 Million Books Sold	124
Does God Heal Animals?	125
Healed Without Realising It	127
Another Solution	128
My Head Bangs Against a Brick Wall	129
Someone's Back Healed When i Entered the House	130
David Hogan Meeting Reached on Time Supernaturally	131
Do We Pray for the Sick?	132
14000 Words Translated in One Evening	136
Attacked on the Street in Zurich	138
Foot Nerve Healed	140
I Fall Out of Bed	141
Needs Met in the Time of the Corona Crisis	142
North Korea Trip 15-24 September 2018	144
The Guides and Drivers	147
The Bus Rides	148
The People of NK	149
Trips	150
Believing for Greater Things	152

FOREWORD

Psalm 103:1-2 Bless the LORD, O my soul: and all that is within me, bless his holy name. Bless the LORD, O my soul, and forget not all his benefits:

I hear the request, "Daddy, tell us a story!" quite a lot recently from my children, so I decided to write down all the stories about my life which I could remember. I have written them down for posterity, as we say. I am not writing an autobiography but rather only the stories where I can see God's hand at work in my life. There are lots of biographical stories which I could have told such as when I cut my nose as a small child trying to carry two milk bottles into the house. I want to glorify God through what I write and I want my children to learn how to live a life of faith, health, provision and a life which seeks to help others in need to find Jesus. I have three wonderful children who are very gifted and I know that the Lord has a great plan for their lives. These stories will help them to see what great things the Lord can do in them and through them. Be blessed my children and anybody else who reads this book.

WHY I WROTE THIS BOOK

Joshua 4:6 That this may be a sign among you, that when your children ask their fathers in time to come, saying, What mean ye by these stones?

Joshua was told to inform his children about God's great works in the past. This is why I wrote this book, in order to remind and encourage my children about how the Lord took care of their dad. I want them to have a practical daily reading with a Bible verse which can help them in their daily lives. I want them to experience daily the miracles of God. I want them to live an exciting life. All of these stories are true and have been personally experienced. Life would be boring if we didn't experience God's miracles daily. It depends on our faith and expectation. Expect little, get little. Look for the Lord in every part of your day and expect his help when problems arise.

I COMMIT MY LIFE TO JESUS AT 11 YEARS OF AGE

Psalm 71:17 O God, thou hast taught me from my youth: and hitherto have I declared thy wondrous works.

As a family we had just moved to a new area in my hometown Burton-on-Trent in England and an elderly woman from a local church knocked on our door one day. She asked my parents if they would like to send us children to the Sunday school. So we started going to Sunday school and I soon learned to love singing the songs and learning the Bible verses off by heart. We sang songs like "Yesterday, today, forever, Jesus is the same.", "What a friend we have in Jesus" and "Jesus bids us shine with a pure clear light."

When I was 10, I was able to go to a boy's summer camp. I remember that I wasn't given any pocket money for the camp but all the other boys in my group put all their money together and shared it out between all of us, so I could have some money. Through the messages and songs, I began to realise that Jesus was calling me to believe in and follow Him. However, I did not make a decision this year.

However, the following year when I was 11, I was especially moved when I say a film called "King of kings" where Jesus was crucified and I realised that He did it for me personally and I wept as I realised that my sin was the reason why he had to die. The camp theme song was "How great Thou art" and this song also spoke to me. Anyway, when the call came for all those who wanted to give their lives to Jesus, I decided that this was the time. We had to go the meeting room after the bonfire which I did, and I prayed with one of the workers. I was so filled with joy that I ran back to my tent in the pitch-black night.

I was praying too for the first time and it felt so good. All in my tent had already fallen asleep so I lay down to sleep. Before I fell asleep, I saw bright lights through the tent wall floating over the tent and I fell asleep. In the morning, I woke up and my hair (I had some in those days ☺) was soaking wet with fresh water and it had not rained. Even though I was young, I realised that the Lord had anointed me and had a great plan for my life. The lights must have been angels, I thought, who were rejoicing over my salvation.

Luke 15:10 Likewise, I say unto you, there is joy in the presence of the angels of God over one sinner that repents.

My life changed for the better as you can read later.

Over 40 years later, I rang one of the leaders of the camp who was in his eighties and thanked him. He was of course moved and happy to hear what I was doing now which included doing camps for prisoners' children.

MAN HEALED OF TINNITUS

Acts 3:6-7 Then Peter said, Silver and gold have I none; but such as I have give I thee: In the name of Jesus Christ of Nazareth rise up and walk. And he took him by the right hand, and lifted him up: and immediately his feet and ankle bones received strength.

I was starting to sing and preach at a breakfast for needy people in Geislingen. One time I went around the tables and shook hands with the people welcoming them and blessing them. I think it is important to show interest in people and not just come and preach to the air and go. I can't stand preachers who avoid contact with the people they are preaching to. Jesus was accessible to people. Anyway, I sang and preached and prayed for people afterwards and left.

Some time later, the pastor sent me an email and said that a miracle happened when I was at the breakfast. A man called Harry had had tinnitus for 20 years but as soon as I shook his hand, he felt an explosion in his ears and his tinnitus left him. His tinnitus was so bad that he had to have a radio in every room to block out the ringing in his ears and the doctor could not help him. His doctor was flabbergasted when he heard his story. 5 years later Harry came and told me that he was still healed. Jesus is the healer but we are his hands of love.

HEALED AS A CHILD

Matthew 2:16 Then Herod, when he saw that he was mocked of the wise men, was exceeding wroth, and sent forth, and slew all the children that were in Bethlehem, and in all the coasts thereof, from two years old and under, according to the time which he had diligently enquired of the wise men.

Satan tried to kill Jesus as a child through Herod. All disease comes from the devil and the devil tried to take my life as a child of 6 months. My parents told me that I contracted pneumonia and in the 1950's this was a big killer. I do not remember the incident of course but it left a shadow on my lung which has caused me problems whenever I had any infection. However, in 2007 I was on a camp for prisoners' children and one night, the Holy Spirit filled my tent like a whirlwind and I breathed in deeply several times and the Lord spoke to me saying, "I am equipping you to minister in worship for these children and I am healing your lungs." We had a fantastic week with the kids and since then I have not had any problems with my lungs and no infections.

With my Dad and brothers David and Derrick

HEALING OF MY BIG TOE

Romans 10:15 And how shall they preach, except they be sent? as it is written, How beautiful are the feet of them that preach the gospel of peace, and bring glad tidings of good things!

For whatever reason, the nail of my right big toe became inflamed and it was very painful. I tried to cut back the nail and treat it myself with creams but to no avail; it just got worse. It became painful to walk and with each step I used to claim my healing in Jesus' name but nothing happened. We see many cases in the Bible where people were sick for a long time and waited for God to heal them. We sometimes need to be patient.

Psalm 40:1 I waited patiently for the LORD; and he inclined unto me, and heard my cry.

Hebrews 6:15 And so, after he had patiently endured, he obtained the promise.

One day I attended a seminar on healing. It was in a big tent and the teaching was really good. The evangelist preaching just taught what the Bible says about healing. In one session he got words of knowledge about people's conditions and one was for me. There were 1000 people in the tent but he pointed in my direction and said, "There is a man over there who has an inflamed big toe and God is healing him right now." Since that time, my toe was completely healed, praise the Lord! We just have to believe and wait patiently.

PROVIDED WITH WORK

Joshua 1:8 This book of the law shall not depart out of thy mouth; but you shall meditate therein day and night, that you may observe to do according to all that is written therein: for then you shall make your way prosperous, and then you shall have good success.

At one time I lost my job in computing and the banks were going through a crisis so I couldn't find any more work. I wondered what to do and I thought about the idea of teaching English. I found a company that was looking for English teachers and applied for a job. I had never taught English in my life and I had no idea about English grammar etc. So the whole thing was a little bit crazy. For the interview I had to prepare a short lesson and present this lesson at the interview. So I did this and prepared some things which I thought would be interesting. The interview went well and they accepted me and began to give me assignments in different companies needing business English. I had started my English career. Then I had a phone call from someone I did not know from a Christian political party. He lived in my village and during the conversation I mentioned that I was out of work and had just started to teach English. He said that he knew a brother in my village who also taught English and so I made contact with him. His school were also looking for teachers. He realised that I needed some help so he took me along to his classes and I learned a lot about how to teach English and a lot about grammar. I went for an interview with his boss and she also decided to take me on despite the fact that I had very little knowledge of the profession and very little experience. Their pay was also much better. Little by little my career as an English trainer was expanding and the Lord was helping me. It also gave me lots of opportunities to share my faith with people. When we discussed hobbies in the class, I talked about the Christian activities I was involved in.

GETTING WORK IN THE FACHHOCHSCHULE

Proverbs 3:6 In all your ways acknowledge Him, and He shall direct your paths.

One day I heard that they were looking for a teacher at the fachhochschule in Stuttgart. In Germany, normally, you need to be qualified to do a job at a fachhochschule but I applied for the job anyway. I went to the interview and the head of the department was an English guy. He took me to lunch and we had a good conversation. Afterwards he told me that he was giving me the job. I was flabbergasted because I had little experience and no qualification but he gave me the job. Why? Some months later I heard what had happened. I was having coffee with some colleagues and the head of the department was also there. He said to a colleague, "Oh, did I ever tell you how Robert came to work here?" I was all ears. "Well", he said, "we needed a teacher but my secretary was on holiday and couldn't send out an ad for the job but somehow Robert heard about the vacancy. He came for an interview and I liked him so I gave him the job. Later we sent out the ad and got many replies from teachers who wanted it but Robert had already been given the job." Wow, I thought, God's ways are mysterious! I had a lot of opportunities to share the Gospel with the students and I was a very popular teacher.

MY FIRST BIBLE

Psalm 119:9 Wherewithal shall a young man cleanse his way? by taking heed thereto according to thy word.

I was 12 years old and after getting saved at the age of 11 I was growing in the Lord. I had one big wish and that was to buy my own nice Bible. I went into a bookshop and found a Bible that I liked and found out the price. I had no money and I received no pocket money because at that time my parents needed all their money to pay off a mortgage for their house. I did not even have a bike or a train set. So how was I going to get money for a Bible? I used to travel to school on the bus so my parents gave me 11 pence per day. Those were the days when there were 12 pence in a shilling and 20 shillings in a pound. My idea was to walk to school and back and save the money for my Bible. I would have to keep it a secret from my parents though. I would have to get up earlier and I would get back home later. However, I did it and even if it rained or snowed, I walked to school which was 5 kilometres away. On the way to school I used to walk past a toyshop with train sets in the window. I used to look at them and see how nice they were but expensive. And anyway, I was walking to school for something more valuable. There were also times when I had the desire for something sweet so I used to buy biscuits or an ice-cream at the school shop.

After 5 months, I had saved enough money for my Bible and I went into the bookshop and bought it. I was so happy to hold this beautiful book in my hands. This book has changed my life and the lives of many people around me. Later I would give free Bibles to prisoners and their children and also to poor people.

I am in the middle

LAUGHED AT IN SCHOOL

Matthew 10:32 Whosoever therefore shall confess me before men, him will I confess also before my Father which is in heaven.

I was 12 years of age and a young Christian. I was doing a Billy Graham correspondence course and I had just written my testimony which was one of the things you had to do. I was serious about following Jesus and I also used to listen to Billy Graham radio broadcasts called "Hour of Decision". I had a little radio with little plug-in earphones and I used to try to tune into the radio station under my bed covers. It always encouraged me in my newly found faith.

I was at school one day and the correspondence course was in my school satchel. We all went out to play rugby and afterwards I came back to have a shower. When I got into the changing rooms a group of boys started chanting a date "20th August 1963..20th August 1963..20th Aug....". This was the date I got saved and one of them had looked into my satchel and read the correspondence course testimony. They decided to make fun of me but actually the whole thing was good for me. Firstly, I was able to share my testimony with all my school comrades all at once and secondly, I was strengthened in my faith through this little bit of persecution. I later became the leader of the school Christian union.

Burton-on-Trent Grammar School

MY AGGRESSION REMOVED

Ecclesiastes 7:9 Be not hasty in your spirit to be angry: for anger resteth in the bosom of fools.

After I got saved at the age of 11, I asked to Lord to help me not be so aggressive. I knew that I had a problem in this area. If someone at school did something bad to me, I used to hit them and got into a lot of fights with boys at school. One day I got into a fight and suddenly this boy and I stood in the school playground surrounded by many other children who wanted to watch the fight. I was quite big so I had a good chance of winning, but at what price? I did not think about this; I just wanted to fight him until he could take no more. Aggression is stupid because it has no regard for the consequences. But suddenly, before I even had a chance to punch the boy, something happened. I suddenly felt something hit my right ear and it hurt. I thought someone had thrown something at me but it was something that fell out of a tree above me. My ear was bleeding and a teacher came and rushed me to hospital where I got stitches in my ear. Maybe this had happened to avoid an even bigger injury.

So I prayed and asked the Lord to remove my aggression and he did. After this I was gentle as a lamb and never hit back when somebody did something bad to me. In fact, I let myself be treated badly many times without resisting.

BAPTISED AT 15 AND PREACHING IN CHURCH AT 16

1 Timothy 4:12 Let no man despise thy youth; but be thou an example of the believers, in word, in conversation, in charity, in spirit, in faith, in purity.

Having been saved at the age of 11, I was a very keen Christian and I was hungry for more of God. I got saved at a boy's camp and I became a camp leader as well. I also served in the Sunday school teaching younger children about Jesus and the Bible. At the age of 15 I realised that I needed to get baptised so I asked to be baptised and it was a wonderful experience. I was also the leader of the Christian union at school. I also helped to start a new Christian coffee bar in the town which we called Link-up. It was here that I first learned to pray out loud in front of other people. It was a wonderful experience and praying together became especially important to me. For the coffee bar I painted a mural on one of the large walls with a sun and many colourful planets being drawn to it. Through Link-up I learned how to lead others to Jesus and we had some really great evenings where people came and got saved. I was growing in the Lord and my church obviously noticed this so I was invited to preach when I turned 16. I can't remember what I preached but I remember that my mother came to church for the first time. She sat at the back. Somebody told me later that she had cried the whole time.

I also led a prayer meeting for all the ministers and pastors in the town. We prayed for revival in the town and we planned an evangelistic crusade which was an enormous success. However, I got criticism from the Pentecostal pastor who thought that I was too young to lead a prayer meeting at 16 years of age. However, the Church of England minister stood up for me and said that I was exactly the right person. How many people have ever got all the pastors and ministers in the town to pray together? I wish this happened more.

THE CHRISTIAN YOUTH CLUB

John 15:8 Herein is my Father glorified, that you bear much fruit; so shall you be my disciples.

When I was 16, I was also a leader at a local Christian youth club and I learned to preach to some really problematic kids who did not really want to hear the Gospel being preached to them. They were wild and noisy but I preached my heart out and I demonstrated the love of Christ to them. I now don't know how I did it but I organised a canal boat holiday for a whole week. This meant renting two boats for a week, one for the boys and one for the girls. I was going to be responsible for cooking along with a few girl helpers. As I write this, I still can't believe that I did all of this. I was able to cook because my parents worked shifts so I had to look after and cook for my two younger brothers. Anyway, I don't remember anybody ever complaining, so I must have done a good job. Of course, my main aim was to win these kids for Jesus. We had some really tough kids who came along. We also had some near disasters. One day both boats were in a canal lock and as the water was falling, both boats were touching and both of them started to tilt and could have sunk. So we had to quickly reverse the process. During this chaos one of the kids dropped his camera in the canal lock.

I remember one evening in particular. After a good meal and a short message to the kids we sat together and started to talk together. One of the guys talked about his stories with his girlfriends but I kept bringing the conversation round to Jesus. We ended up talking the whole night and afterwards I made breakfast and then the holiday was over. In the evening, we had a coffee bar session with a good Gospel band and a speaker. Some of the kids who were on the holiday came along and as the speaker made an appeal for people to receive Jesus some of them stepped forward and received Jesus into their lives. One of them was this difficult kid with all his girlfriend stories. Later he became the leader of Youth for Christ in the whole area and many came to Jesus through him.

A COFFEE TABLE APPEARS

Luke 6:38 Give, and it shall be given unto you; good measure, pressed down, and shaken together, and running over, shall men give into your bosom. For with the same measure that ye mete withal it shall be measured to you again.

One weekend I had to move and as I was going to have my smallgroup over for Christmas dinner I thought it would be nice to have another coffee table. I went on an outing with my church and the pastor's fiancée forgot to punch her ticket and got fined 80 Swiss francs. I felt led to pay the fine and tried to do it secretly but she found out. Anyway, I went home that night and outside my apartment door was a coffee table. I took it into my apartment. No one knows how it got there so the Lord must have read my thoughts and given it me. It came in useful for the Christmas dinner. Then on the Monday I got a rebate from my landlord of 88 Euros (130 Swiss francs)!!! The Lord blesses us when we bless others. :)

HOW I BECAME A SOFTWARE ENGINEER

1 Samuel 2:30 .... they that honour me I will honour, and they that despise me shall be lightly esteemed.

After I graduated from the University of Birmingham with an Engineering Production degree, I started to look for a job at Lucas Electrical Ltd. in Birmingham. I was moved from department to department to get to know what they did. I was put into a sales engineering department where they tested products among other things. I was not really excited about any of the departments where I had worked and wondered if engineering was the right job for me. I was often sent down to the shop floor with a list of products which they needed for testing. However, I found out somehow that not all the products were being tested but rather stolen. They were all car components like starters, alternators and lamps. The employers were either using them for their own needs or giving them to friends and relatives. So the next time I was asked to go and fetch products from the shop floor, I refused. I did not want to compromise my Christian principles but I also realised that it had consequences. Shortly after this, I was informed that the manager wanted to see me. I thought that this would be the end of my career. The manager was named Mr. K. And he was feared by everybody. I went to see him and sat down. "Mr. Young", he said, "I've heard that you are refusing orders." "Well", I replied, "if you mean refusing to steal then you are right." He looked a bit shocked. "I know what you mean Mr. Young", he said, "but these sorts of things are contained in the budget." "Well", I said, "I am a Christian and stealing is against my Christian principles whether it is budgeted or not." He realised that he was not going to get anywhere with me so he said something I was not expecting. "Okay Mr. Young", he said, "I understand your point of view. You see my brother is a minister of a church and he sees thing like you see them. I have a suggestion. There is a new department which is looking for someone to do programming. Would you be interested? If so, then I can transfer you there. Is that okay with you?" Of course I agreed, being relieved that he was treating me fairly. The same day, his boss came to me and tugged on my jacket and said, "Mr. Young, I admire your courage in saying what you did." And he continued in a quieter tone, "I have been too involved for too long a time to do anything about it." Wow! What a confession.

Anyway, I was moved to this new department and I learned how to program and work with and design databases etc. My new boss was the best boss I have ever had and he inspired me a lot. I had finally found a job where I was fulfilled and it also finally led me to Germany.

FREE PHYSICS TUITION

Luke 17:16-18 And fell down on his face at his feet, giving him thanks: and he was a Samaritan. And Jesus answering said, Were there not ten cleansed? but where are the nine? There are not found that returned to give glory to God, save this stranger.

I always wanted to become a missionary. An older brother gave me some advice and said that I should get a university degree so I could go anywhere in the world and preach the Gospel. So I chose a general engineering course at university but I needed 2 C's and an E in maths, physics and chemistry to qualify. However my physics was extremely poor. I was so involved in Christian activities like the Christian youth club, the coffee bar and the school Christian union and studying was taking second place. However, my physics teacher Mr. S. knew all this and felt he had to somehow help me. He was also a Christian and extremely popular with the pupils. So, he decided to invite me to his home, let his wife cook me meals and he gave me free physics tuition. Have you ever heard of such a thing? I have never heard of anyone doing this before. Anyway, it worked, and I got 2 C's and a D, which was better than the requirement. Without his help, my life would have been completely different and I would never have gone to Germany.

Recently, I decided to try to contact Mr. S. And thank him for what he did. I rang him and found that he and his wife were well and still active in his local church although they were in their seventies. He was moved to hear my thanks and to hear what had happened to me. It is good to thank those who have changed our lives through their loving gestures.

I GET A CAR FOR CHRISTMAS

Proverbs 19:17 He that hath pity upon the poor lends unto the LORD; and that which he hath given will he pay him again.

I was out of work and during this time the Lord put it on my heart to help people in need because I was now realising how they felt. At Christmas, I had the idea to make food packets and give them to tramps that I found in Stuttgart. My car had recently given up the ghost but I had no money, so getting a new car seemed hopeless. Somebody offered me 1000€ to buy a car but I told them that that was too little.

So, on Christmas Day I prepared a lot of food packets with chicken sandwiches, fruit and vegetables, chocolate, a drink and also some christian literature. I went to the morning service at church but told no one about what I was doing. However, there was a new man in the church who had heard us sing and preach in Stuttgart in the open air. I got talking to him and told him what I was going to do. He asked if he could come so I took him with me. I wasn't sure whether or not he was saved but I told him that we would always present the people with the food packet by saying that it was from Jesus. We walked all over Stuttgart and found men and women tramps everywhere; in the toilets, under bridges and on the streets begging. The man with me was very interested and he gave the food packets to the people in the name of Jesus. During this time he shared that he was in the process of moving and wanted to sell some things. One of them was a car of his. As soon as I heard that, I asked him how much he wanted for the car and he said 1000€ which was, of course, the sum that someone had offered me so I told him that I would buy it off him. So the person gave me the money and the Lord had given me a car on Christmas Day.

We finished giving out all the food packets and I invited him back to my flat for a traditional English Christmas dinner.

THE 21ST FOOD PACKET

Proverbs 22:9 He that hath a bountiful eye shall be blessed; for he giveth of his bread to the poor.

Another Christmas I decided to distribute food packets again. This time I decided to make 20 packets because this seemed to be the number of food packets that one could distribute to tramps in Stuttgart in about 3 hours because that was about the number of tramps you find on Christmas day. But I found that I had enough buns and things for 21 packets so I made 21.

I went again with the man who sold me his car the year before. We spent hours looking for tramps and ended up distributing 20 food packets. However, we had one packet left and wondered where we were going to find someone who needed it. Suddenly, I saw a man who must have been about 60 walking from rubbish bin to rubbish bin on the Königstrasse in Stuttgart looking for something to eat. What a pitiful sight, I thought. We approached him and gave him the packet in the name of Jesus. You should have seen his face! He thanked us profusely.

The Lord knew the need of this man and caused me to make 21 packets instead of 20. I pray that this man will end up receiving Jesus. We are just one link in the chain. We may sow something in someone's heart and then another reaps the harvest at another point in time. At least this man was able to enjoy a hearty meal on Christmas day.

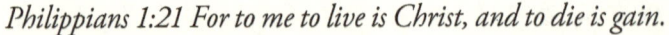
CAN'T LIVE WITHOUT YOU JESUS

Philippians 1:21 For to me to live is Christ, and to die is gain.

I was out of work and sometimes so depressed by the situation that I would sit down and cry. However, during this time I learnt that money and possessions are not as important as Jesus. Only he can give happiness and true satisfaction. It was during this time that I wrote a song called: **"Can't live without You Jesus"**.

Chorus
Can't live without you Jesus; wouldn't want to try.
Can't live without you Jesus; that's not a lie.
Can't live without you Jesus, You died for me.
You gave Your life to set me free.
Upon the cross at Calvary.

Sure I've tried other ways to find real peace.
To fill that emptiness in me.
But You found me and now my search has ceased.
Just knowing You is all I need.

Chorus
You said You are the way, the truth, the life.
Come to seek and save the lost like me.
And You found me and brought me to Your light.
And now I'll live eternally.

Chorus

OPPOSITION FROM A PROJECT LEADER

Matthew 5:43-45 You have heard that it hath been said, you shalt love your neighbour, and hate your enemy. But I say unto you, Love your enemies, bless them that curse you, do good to them that hate you, and pray for them which despitefully use you, and persecute you; That you may be the children of your Father which is in heaven: for he maketh his sun to rise on the evil and on the good, and sendeth rain on the just and on the unjust.

I had started a new job in Zurich, Switzerland in April and it was going well. The colleagues were very nice and the work was exactly what I liked to do and I was really coming up with some good ideas. However, in August something happened. My teamleader asked for a private talk with me and told me that the project leader had told him that he thought I was dragging my feet at work. My teamleader told me that he had contradicted him and told him that he was satisfied with my work and that I was doing a good job. Anyway, it appears that the project leader was talking to a few people about me. I was a bit shocked but I just kept calm about this situation and acted normally. That evening I went home and read the verse for the day which was:

Genesis 26:3 Sojourn in this land, and I will be with thee, and will bless thee;

This was a great blessing to me and showed that everything would be fine. I went camping for a week in Germany on the Indian camp for children of prisoners. When I came back, I found that the project leader had been relieved of his post and had to seek a new job. I did not gloat about it but rather I wrote him an email to say that I was sad about him losing his post and I wished him all the best for his future. Indeed, he found a new job and when he left, I was the only one to give him a leaving present of 2 bottles of good wine and a copy of my book. As Jesus said, "..bless them that curse you."

IT'S RAINING MONEY

Philippians 4:19 But my God shall supply all your need according to his riches in glory by Christ Jesus.

I was out of work and had no support from the State. I was at the beginning of starting a career as an English trainer but I was not yet earning enough to live on. It was the time of Hartz 4 in Germany which was the name for the social security system. However, I used to say that I lived from Philippians 4 *"...my God shall suplly all your need..."* and He proved it to me many times. I had never been so dependant on God, so in a way it was a useful experience.

Here are a few examples of what happened. Once I was driving to the church Bible and prayer evening. I was praying in the car and I was rather direct in my prayer. I prayed, "Lord, I have had a lot of expenses: I had to buy a new car battery and I drove to Magdeburg to do a week of evangelism in Smart cars there which cost a lot of petrol money. Now I have no money and I need money now. Thank You Lord, in Jesus' name. Amen." The Lord has no problem if we pray like this.

Anyway, I arrived at church and had only just walked through the door when an elderly sister, whose name I did not even know at that time, walked up to me and put an envelope into my hand. Later, I opened the envelope and there was 200€ in it! The Lord had answered my prayer before I had even prayed it. He had told this sister to give me 200€.

Some time later, my doorbell rang and it was a brother from another church who was also an English trainer and had taken me to his lessons a few times. He told me that he had just drawn money from an ATM. Suddenly the Lord spoke to him and told him to bring the money to me. He handed the money over to me: 350€

One day there was an anonomous envelope in my letterbox with 50€ in it and a card with a rainbow on it and the verse which had accompanied me to Germany:

> *Genesis 12:2-3 And I will make of thee a great nation, and I will bless thee, and make thy name great; and thou shalt be a blessing: And I will bless them that bless thee, and curse him that curseth thee: and in thee shall all families of the earth be blessed.*

I had people who put money into my hand and I even found money notes lying on the ground. I can honestly say that I was never in desperate need and I was always able to support my children.

In 2010, I wanted to pay for something at a shop but my card was rejected because my bank account was empty. I had been out of work for several months. I looked up to the Lord and asked, "Lord, what are you going to do now?". I went to the prayer meeting where I lead the worship. Before the meeting started, a lady gave me an envelope. I thought it was a letter, but when I looked inside the envelope, there were two 100 Swiss francs notes in it. Later the lady told me that the Lord had told her to give me the money but she didn't know why. I did though.

BLESSED WITH CLOTHES

Matthew 6:28-30 And why take ye thought for raiment? Consider the lilies of the field, how they grow; they toil not, neither do they spin: And yet I say unto you, That even Solomon in all his glory was not arrayed like one of these. Wherefore, if God so clothe the grass of the field, which today is, and tomorrow is cast into the oven, shall he not much more clothe you, O ye of little faith?

I was still not very financially stable so I had to be careful about what I bought. Once I wanted a nice black blazer and I looked in the shops but I decided it was too expensive. The Lord loves us and he knows what we desire and because He loves us and he wants to surprise us with his loving kindness. I went to my family on Sunday to have breakfast before church and my ex-wife said that somebody had given her a brand-new Boss black blazer and if it fitted me I could have it. It was exactly my size so the Lord had fulfilled my wish.

Another time I also needed a black woollen zip-up pullover but again I decided not to buy one. I taught English at a local company and one day I was there and they presented me with a promotion gift: a black woollen zip-up pullover.

A HITCHHIKER SAVES MY DAY

Hebrews 13:2 Be not forgetful to entertain strangers: for thereby some have entertained angels unawares.

I had moved from Birmingham to Stevenage where I bought a mobile home to live in. It was on a plot of land and had a living room, a kitchen, a bathroom and a bedroom. It had a stove which heated the central heating. I was comfortable and happy.

It was winter and I was driving back after a great weekend's conference where I had led the worship. It was nearly midnight and was snowing. Suddenly, I heard the Lord speaking to me and He said, "You will soon see a man at the side of the road thumbing for a lift. Stop and pick him up and take him home with you." Sure enough I soon saw a man thumbing a lift. I stopped, opened the door and invited him to come in. I told him that God had told me to take him home with me. Surprisingly, he did not refuse or make any comment. At the time I did not consider the strangeness of this situation but now I ask myself why he let himself be taken to my home? He seemed to be around 50 and he did not say much. He said something about moving from place to place doing odd jobs.

Anyway, we arrived at my mobile home and I got a shock as I opened the door. Water poured out because the heating pipes had burst and there were 6 inches of water in the mobile home. I had no idea what to do and it was about 1am so how could I get help at this hour? However, the next surprise was that this man had a tool bag with him and without comment he got down to fixing the pipes. He seemed to work very quickly and I was able to start a fire in the stove and the heating was in operation again. I made some food and we sat round the stove and ate it. As I looked into his face, I thought he looked very much like my father.

The man slept on my sofa and the next morning I drove him to the station, gave him 5 pounds and that was the last I saw of him. Some friends tell me they think I was helped by an angel. I am not sure, but all I can say is that the Lord helped me through this man.

The pipes were perfectly repaired and I did not need any other work done afterwards. The mobile home dried out well and in the summer, I sold the mobile home and moved to Germany.

I WIN AN OVEN

Ecclesiastes 5:19 Every man also to whom God hath given riches and wealth, and hath given him power to eat thereof, and to take his portion, and to rejoice in his labour; this is the gift of God.

I was living in my mobile home in Stevenage. I had a gas stove where the gas came from a canister but it was defect and I needed a new oven. I went to a shop and bought a new oven although I did not really have much money. When I was paying for the oven the shop assistant said that they had a competition and if I guessed correctly how long a gas canister would last for a family of four then I would get my money back. So I took a guess and paid for the oven and forgot all about it. However, about a month later I received a letter saying that I had won the competition and I was getting my money back. The Lord is good.

JOHANNA IS BORN

Leviticus 6:27 And they shall put my name upon the children of Israel; and I will bless them.

Johanna

My wife was expecting our first child Johanna (God is merciful) and we had decided to have the baby at home with two midwives present. However, just a few days before Johanna was expected she was still in the feet-down position and not in the head-down position. If this stayed like this she would have to be delivered in a clinic because of complications. So I decided to pray. Susanne sat on the sofa and I prayed and then commanded the baby to turn. Immediately, Susanne felt the baby do a flip and she was then in the head-down position. Years later I tell my daughter that she obeyed me at least once in her life ☺.

My father with Johanna

Johanna Olivia Young was then born at home a few days later and it was a wonderful experience even if it did take a long time. After the birth, Johanna did not want to sleep and she kept us up all night playing with her.

I OVERCOME MY FEAR OF WATER ETC.

Psalm 34.11 Come, ye children, hearken unto me: I will teach you the fear of the LORD.

I must have had a bad time at the age of 14. Maybe it was puberty or problems at home. I still had a fear of water and could not swim. Going to the swimming baths at that age was a horror. However, one day somebody pushed me into the water and suddenly my fear left me and I enjoyed swimming.

I had another problem and that was that I sucked my thumb which shows that I felt insecure. Anyway, I was ashamed of this habit and I asked the Lord to help me to stop it.

I went to the boy's camp again where I got saved and we played a chasing game. I grabbed for the pullover of one of the camp leaders and he ran off which then broke the ring finger of my left hand. I was taken to hospital where a nurse just bound up the hand with a bandage without fixing the broken bone. This left my finger crooked even to this day. However, with the hand all bound up I was unable to suck my thumb so I lost the habit which was an answer to prayer.

MY RIGHT KNEE GETS HEALED

Job 4:4 Thy words have upholden him that was falling, and thou hast strengthened the feeble knees.

One day I was at work in Zurich and I suddenly felt my right knee give way and I felt pain. I was hardly able to walk or to put weight on the knee. I somehow managed to get home but I wondered how I was going to walk to work the next day. I prayed for my knee and realised that I needed prayer support. The Godtube site in internet had a prayer wall where you could enter prayer requests and other users could pray for you. Some time later I got up to get a drink and suddenly noticed that my knee was healed and that I had no more pain and the knee felt strong. I was encouraged and I thought about a colleague's cat which was dying. I thought, "If prayer worked for me then it could work for this cat." So I entered a prayer request in the prayer wall and prayed for the cat.

The next day I told my colleague what had happened and he shared that his cat was now eating and seemed to be improving. The cat survived and now, after a year, my knee is also still fine.

I GIVE MY CAR AWAY

Mark 10:21 Then Jesus beholding him loved him, and said unto him, One thing thou lackest: go thy way, sell whatsoever thou hast, and give to the poor, and thou shalt have treasure in heaven: and come, take up the cross, and follow me.

I gave up riding motorbikes because I had fallen off three times already so I decided to buy a car again. A colleague sold me his nice Ford Cortina which looked good and had nice comfortable seats. However, I had to take out a bank loan to buy it.

One Sunday we had a visiting Pastor at my church who came with his whole family. His car had a problem and was virtually a write-off. I felt strongly that the Lord wanted me to give him my car, so without thinking too much about it I gave him the keys to my car and told him that it was now his car. The most embarassing part was having to explain to my colleagues and family why I didn't have a car anymore. Everybody thought I was crazy. I also still had to pay off the debt for the car. I had literally given away all that I possessed and more. I had to then travel everywhere by bus and train.

However, not too long after that, the Lord helped me to buy my brand new dream car; a red MG Metro.

"TAKE ONE STEP BACK!"

John 10:27-28 My sheep hear my voice, and I know them, and they follow me. And I give unto them eternal life; and they shall never perish, neither shall any man pluck them out of my hand.

I was on an Indian camp for prisoners' children one year and was helping to wash the dishes. One of the sisters brought some boiling water in a large pot. Suddenly, I heard the Lord whisper to me, "Take one step back!" I instantly did this and suddenly the sister tripped and the whole pot of water fell at my feet but not one drop fell on me. However, if I had not quickly stepped out of the way, the whole of the boiling water would have fallen over my body and I hate to think of how I would have been injured. I have learned to hear the voice of the Lord and to obey immediately.

Another time recently, I was parking my car in Stuttgart in a carpark. I drove up behind another car and the entrance was on a bit of a slope. Again I heard the voice of the Lord saying, "Don't park too near to that car in front of you!" So I stopped about 4 metres away. Suddenly, after collecting the carpark ticket, the car in front of me shot back and stopped just in inches away from my bumper. If I had been nearer, my car would have been badly damaged. It is good to hear God's voice.

I WRITE MY FIRST BOOK "JESUS BEHIND BARS"

Nehemiah 2:18 Then I told them of the hand of my God which was good upon me; as also the king' words that he had spoken unto me. And they said, Let us rise up and build. So they strengthened their hands for this good work.

Because of the 20-year anniversary of the Jesus-Group prison ministry, I decided to write a book containing many testimonies of the work. When I had the vision to write this book, it was not possible because my old PC was not capable of performing such an enormous task. The software was too old and the performance was too low. I went into a computer shop and looked at the prices. I realised that I was not financially in the position to buy a computer. So I prayed: "Lord, if You want me to buy a new PC then please show me." The next day I received an unexpected cheque for 300 English pounds in the post. It was enough to buy a new PC!

Apart from this I also needed a USB-stick. Also here I experienced God's help. A customer was so satisfied with my translation work that he gave me a new USB-stick.

I started to work on the book in June 2006. After just one month I had already written 50 pages. But then I lost all interest. I had a block and I was no longer able to work on the book. In August I asked people to pray for me that I would receive motivation to finish the book. Afterwards I received motivation again to finish the book so that I finished it in September. Praise the Lord!

I START WORKING IN THE JESUS-GROUP PRISON MINISTRY

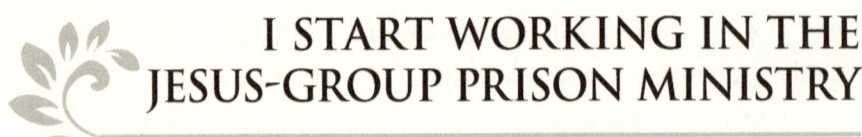

Matthew 25:35-36 For I was a hungry, and ye gave me meat: I was thirsty, and ye gave me drink: I was a stranger, and ye took me in: Naked, and ye clothed me: I was sick, and ye visited me: I was in prison, and ye came unto me.

I came to Germany in 1985 and in 1990 I was led to join the Volksmission in Stuttgart-Zuffenhausen. When I moved to Germany the Lord told me that He would bless me and make me a blessing. I heard that the church had a prison ministry. I was extremely interested in such a ministry and so I asked the Lord to show me if it was his will for me to be involved. The sign I asked for was that someone would come and ask me if I was interested in working in the prison. The following Sunday I was surprised how often the word "prison" was mentioned in the service. After the service, Werner Mathes came to me and asked me exactly the question that I had asked from God as a sign. I joyfully answered "Yes!" immediately. I was completely new in the church so I was surprised that he asked me such a question. As a reason for this Werner said that they had been praying for a long time for an English person to start an English Jesus-Group. Therefore, I was an answer to prayer. It took some months for the official permit, but then I went to my first Jesus-Group in Stammheim. It was my first time in a prison and I just had to weep as I saw these men without hope. But Jesus is our hope, and it is great to see how the Gospel of Jesus changes the lives of men in prison. I started my ministry in the German group. Later, in 1993, I started the first English group with Detlef Guderian which has continued strongly to this day.

JESUS IS WAITING

Revelation 3:20 Behold, I stand at the door, and knock: if any man hears my voice, and open the door, I will come in to him, and will sup with him, and he with me.

It is always something extremely dramatic when one enters Stammheim prison. After you have entered the main gate you have to go through up to 10 more gates in order to get to the place where the prisoners are. One evening I came to the floor where the showers were. The inmates in my group work every day. In the evening they can take a shower. When I arrived, some of them were still in the shower. One of the guards knocked on the door and cried out:

"Hello ... hurry up ... Jesus is waiting!"

How true! Revelation 3, 21 says that Jesus is waiting in front of the door of our hearts for us to open the door and let Him in. Jesus wants fellowship with us!

PRISONERS GET SAVED!

Luke 4:18 The Spirit of the Lord is upon me, because he hath anointed me to preach the gospel to the poor; he hath sent me to heal the broken-hearted, to preach deliverance to the captives, and recovering of sight to the blind, to set at liberty them that are bruised,

On one evening as we were singing and I was playing the guitar, suddenly two of the prisoners walked towards me. I wondered what they wanted. When they stood where I was, they asked me to pray with them. They wanted to publicly confess Jesus and receive Him as the Lord of their lives. They were both Muslims.

On one evening I went to the group quite depressed. I was a long time out of work and had financial problems. On this evening I prayed to the Lord and asked Him to show me that He was with me. It was a nice evening in prison. I preached a short message and gave my testimony about how I found Jesus as a child. When I asked if anyone wanted to give their life to Jesus, three men came to me and knelt down and prayed to receive Jesus. The Lord gave me the sign that He was with me.

PRISONERS DELIVERED FROM NICOTINE

John 8:36 If the Son therefore shall make you free, ye shall be free indeed.

A prisoner came to me one evening and wanted me to pray for him. He told me that he had tried to give up smoking but he was not able to. I then prayed for him. The following week, he told me what happened: "I went back to my cell and had the desire to smoke a cigarette. As I put the cigarette to my mouth, I suddenly started to cough. It was impossible to smoke. The coughing lasted a whole week. Afterwards, I had no more desire for cigarettes." Praise the Lord!

The Lord often works differently to what we expect. Another prisoner also asked me to pray for his cigarette addiction. However, this prisoner did not get a cough; but instead, he had pains in the chest. This lasted until he finally had no more desire for cigarettes.

PRISONERS BECOME PREACHERS

Mark 5:19 Howbeit Jesus suffered him not, but saith unto him, Go home to thy friends, and tell them how great things the Lord hath done for thee, and hath had compassion on thee.

I mentioned once in the Jesus-Group, that my aim was to help prisoners to be inspired to preach the word of God themselves. One evening I came to the group late. I had forgotten my pass so I had to drive back home to get it.

When I finally arrived in the group room to begin my work, I couldn't believe my eyes. The prisoners had set up a pulpit and two prisoners were preaching the word of God. They were also prepared and had written down notes in their cells of what was on their heart.

The other prisoners were listening attentively. After the message, a Muslim came to the front and gave his life to Jesus. Since this evening, it is usual for one of the prisoners to preach a short message every week. I am always astonished how profound these messages are.

One day in the week, it is allowed to invite other prisoners into your cell. Two of the prisoners used this opportunity in order to hold services in their cells. D. invited five men. Before his conversion they did all sorts of other things in the cell. But, on this day, he said to them: "We won't have baseball today; I'm going to preach to you." He did this and prayed for the men afterwards. D. said that he felt God working very powerfully as he was preaching. All the men in his cell had shed tears.

Since then he has held a service in his cell every week. In this way God makes workers out of lost sheep, even in prison. All praise to our Lord Jesus Christ for this!

RAINBOWS – A NEW JOB AND A NEW CHURCH

Revelation 4:3 And he that sat was to look upon like a jasper and a sardine stone: and there was a rainbow round about the throne, in sight like unto an emerald.

Rainbows have always been a sign to me that the Lord is with me and guiding me. I had not had a software engineering job for about 4 years when suddenly, on my birthday, the verse for the day was:

Deuteronomy 28:12 The LORD shall open unto thee his good treasure, the heaven to give the rain unto thy land in his season, and to bless all the work of thine hand: and thou shalt lend unto many nations, and thou shalt not borrow.

On this day I was offered a new job in Zürich. As I was informing an English class of mine that I was leaving, a rainbow appeared outside and I took it as another confirmation that this was the job the Lord wanted me to have.

Me in Zürich

So I moved to Zürich but I needed a new church. I had heard a Zürich pastor at a conference, so I decided to join that church. When I was there, I asked the Lord to confirm that this was the right church. Suddenly, a rainbow appeared near the church so I took that as a confirmation. It has since been confirmed. I was able to help in the setting up of a new English service and I am doing a lot of translation for the church.

# MY HOUSE GETS BROKEN INTO

Luke 11.11-13 If a son shall ask bread of any of you that is a father, will he give him a stone? or if he ask a fish, will he for a fish give him a serpent? Or if he shall ask an egg, will he offer him a scorpion? If ye then, being evil, know how to give good gifts unto your children: how much more shall your heavenly Father give the Holy Spirit to them that ask him?

I had a house in England and after being away on holiday I got home one day to find that the front door was open and someone had broken in and stolen a lot of things. They had left the house in a total mess with everything thrown all over the floor. My guitar was stolen, my radio/cassette player, money and lots of other valuables. I was most upset about my guitar and radio/cassette player. So I prayed and asked the Lord to return those two objects. I reported the break-in to the police and they soon found the youths who had done it but all they were able to recover were the guitar and the radio/cassette player. Specific prayer gets a specific answer.

FOOD PROVIDED

Matthew 6:8 Be not ye therefore like unto them: for your Father knoweth what things ye have need of, before ye ask him.

I was walking to work one day and I kept thinking about how much I would like to eat a ham sandwich. Where I worked there were croissants and buns put out for the workers for free but NO ham sandwiches. Anyway, when I got to work and went to fetch a croissant, I saw a wrapped ham sandwich lying on the top of the croissants so I took it and thanked the Lord that he sees our desires and fulfils them.

Another day we went up to a restaurant with colleagues on the hill near where I live. During the meal I observed a mother who brought her daughter up the hill to see the nice view of the Lake of Zürich. Her daughter was in a wheelchair and it was obvious that she was undergoing treatment for cancer. I felt led to pay for their meal and put some money in the wheelchair while they were in the restroom for a short time but somehow they knew that I had done it so I got talking to them and said I would pray for her daughter. Anyway, the big surprise was that my team leader paid for my meal later so the Lord blessed me too.

VARIOUS PROPHECIES

1 Corinthians 14:3 But he that prophesieth speaketh unto men to edification, and exhortation, and comfort

Prophecy has played a big part in my life. When we were considering joining a new church in Stuttgart, I went to the Bible study and prayer meeting and during this there was a prophecy which I received for myself. It said that someone there was like a blocked hosepipe and God wanted to unblock it and flow through this person. I felt that I was blocked and not free to serve the Lord. I went forward for prayer and the Lord showed me through this that this was the right church. Later I was to be called to help in the Jesus-Group prison ministry.

Another time I felt called to help with the Café 47 work so I went there to see if the Lord would direct me. When I was there, a brother pointed to me and said, "This is your missionary field!" He was prophesying and it was the confirmation I needed. Sadly, the work was hard and we did not see much fruit, but much seed was sown in this time and it will surely bear fruit.

Another time, I was driving to the worship and blessing evening and I prayed, "Lord, please show me tonight if I should spend more time evangelising." Near the end of the service there was an exceptionally long prophecy and I knew the Lord was speaking to me. It said that someone would be used in evangelism and the Lord would equip them. I felt in my spirit that I was meant and I wept and went forward for prayer. To be honest, I don't remember all the details of the prophecy. Soon afterwards I received invitations to preach in different places such as breakfasts for poor people or senior citizen meetings etc. I was already preaching in prisons. Also people were moved by my preaching and got saved.

Recently, in Zürich, someone had a word for me who did not know me. They said that I would start a new work for the poor. This was also confirmed in my church in Germany. Soon afterwards I got invitations to preach at breakfasts for the poor and I have now started to work for a ministry in Zürich which works amongst the poor and needy in Zürich.

THE LORD GIVES ME MY DESIRES

> *Psalm 37:4 Delight thyself also in the LORD; and he shall give you the desires of your heart.*

I believe the Lord is with us all the while and he looks for ways to bless us. Here are a few examples that come to mind.

I found a new job in Germany and I was organising my departure from England. I happened to need a nice briefcase so I went into a shop to buy one. However, I heard the Lord speak to me saying; "Don't buy this briefcase." So I obeyed.

I did a leaving do for my colleagues and they presented me with a leaving present. A black briefcase!

I was out of work at one time but teaching some English but I was still short of money. There was a film that I wanted to see at the cinema and I also needed some relaxation. However, I stood outside the cinema and wondered if I should spend my money for the cinema. As I was wondering, a student of mine suddenly appeared and offered me a complementary cinema ticket so I was able to see the film without paying.

Another time during this financially difficult time my sofa and armchair were old and worn out. I silently wished I had some decent furniture. My family was moving to a smaller place and I was offered the leather sofa and armchairs which were in an exceptionally good condition.

SIDE HEALED AFTER FALL

Isaiah 53:5 But he was wounded for our transgressions, he was bruised for our iniquities: the chastisement of our peace was upon him; and with his stripes we are healed.

I was on an Indian camp once for prisoners' children and I had to act in a little play for the children. In this play I get attacked and someone jumped on me. When I fell to the ground, I hurt myself and then one of the leaders sat on my rib cage and it really hurt. I was injured but I was not sure how badly.

When I was at home after the camp I was still in pain. The pain in my side disturbed my sleep and I had problems breathing and it got worse every day.

I went to a breakfast for poor people and took a Nigerian pastor with me. He was going to preach and I was to sing a few songs. After the breakfast, I asked him to pray for my problem. As he prayed, I felt as if an icy knife was cutting into my side. But, the next day, I was healed and free of pain or discomfort. Praise Jesus!

FOUR WOMEN TRY TO GET ME THE SACK

Isaiah 54:17 No weapon that is formed against thee shall prosper; and every tongue that shall rise against thee in judgment thou shalt condemn. This is the heritage of the servants of the LORD, and their righteousness is of me, saith the LORD.

I moved to Stevenage in England and had a new job as a team leader. The problem is that a woman colleague thought she should have got the job. Also, apparently, she and other colleagues did not like my Christian values and felt threatened.

One day my boss called me into his office and asked me if it was true what four women colleagues had complained to him about. Apparently, they had made up a story about me harassing them and being discriminating towards them. I explained that it was not true. He realised what was going on and he told me not to worry.

Within a month, all four women had left the company. The main problem woman got a bad work report and was fired. I do not gloat about this but it shows that criticising a child of God is a dangerous thing. These people were touching the apple of God's eye. Indeed *"No weapon formed against us shall prosper."*

SUSANNE'S HEALINGS

Mark 16:18 They shall take up serpents; and if they drink any deadly thing, it shall not hurt them; they shall lay hands on the sick, and they shall recover.

We were on a conference and Susanne was expecting Johanna. After one of the meetings I decided to pray for Susanne. She was concerned about a hip problem, especially with the approaching birth. I made her sit down on a chair and lifted her legs to see if they were the same length. They were not the same length as a result of the hip problem. Anyway, I prayed for her healing in the name of Jesus and she suddenly felt one of her legs grow out. I only had my hands under her legs. They were now the same length and she was healed. The birth happened later without complications.

For some time Susanne suffered from a shoulder problem. One day I came into the kitchen where she was and the Lord told me to take her hand and pull her arm. I did this without warning and she was healed. The problem disappeared.

THE FIRST TIME I HEARD GOD'S VOICE

2 Kings 6:5-7 But as one was felling a beam, the axe head fell into the water: and he cried, and said, Alas, master! for it was borrowed. And the man of God said, Where fell it? And he shewed him the place. And he cut down a stick, and cast it in thither; and the iron did swim. Therefore said he, Take it up to thee. And he put out his hand, and took it.

I was about 17 and I was a leader at a summer camp for the first time. I was responsible for a group of boys. We slept in dormitories and not in tents in those days. We had a camp on the coast in England. I had a diving mask and one of the boys asked to borrow it when they went to the beach. They came back and told me the bad news that they had lost the mask in the water and couldn't find it again. I was sad but suddenly the Lord said to me, "Walk to the beach and keep walking straight on and you will find the mask." I obeyed and sure enough I walked exactly to where the mask was. I showed the boys when I got back and it was a good sign to them that Jesus is real. You think God is not interested in small things? Well, in the Bible verse above he helped Elisha to retrieve an axe head from the water, didn't He? It was the first time that I had heard from the Lord. I was to recognise his voice more in the future.

TERROR ACT STOPPED IN GERMANY

Isaiah 54:14 In righteousness shalt thou be established: thou shalt be far from oppression; for thou shalt not fear: and from terror; for it shall not come near thee.

When the Football European cup was in Germany I was appointed as the prayer coordinator for Kickoff 2006 which was the evangelisation programme going on during the competition. So I was given a lot of responsibility.

I was driving in my car one day and suddenly the Lord spoke to me and said: "Germany is being attacked by men from Lebanon with bombs." I took this warning seriously and I knew I had to pray so I stopped the car and prayed against this attack that it would be stopped.

The next day I heard on the news that 2 case bombs had been found at train stations but they had not gone off for some reason. I then prayed that the men would be caught. One of the men was soon caught but the other one was on the run. At this point I told my daughter Jessica what had happened but she said, "But Daddy, one of them is still on the run." "Yes", I said, "but you wait." Sure enough, the other man was caught the next day. Both men were later given life sentences and it was confirmed that both bombs had a mistake which stopped them going off.

I believe the Lord hindered the whole thing through prayer, not just through my prayer but maybe through others too. Prayer is a powerful thing. God works through our prayers.

Later I asked the Lord why he had informed me. He answered, "Well, you were the prayer coordinator for kickoff2006 so you needed to be informed so you could pray."

GOD PREPARES ME FOR CHURCH TRANSLATION WORK

Romans 8:28 And we know that all things work together for good to them that love God, to them who are the called according to his purpose.

In another story I tell how, after not finding work as a software engineer, I got into teaching English. I also got into doing translation for money. The Lord provided me with quite a lot of assignments. However, there is a lot about this work which I had to learn. These times were not easy and it was hard to earn a good living.

Later I got a new software engineer job in Zürich so I moved there and joined a new church. Soon the church decided to start a new English speaking international church meeting. There was a lot of translation that needed doing and the pastor's English was not perfect. I volunteered to help with the translation and every week I send the pastor a list of his English mistakes so he can improve. So, I have a licence to criticise the pastor ☺.

I am also now translating the pastor's books into English and in record time. I prayed to work fast and I translated the first book in 10 days.

It didn't occur to me at once, but later I realised that the Lord had prepared me for this work. What I regarded as a hard time was his preparation time for me.

THE OLDEST WOMAN IN BADEN WUERTTEMBERG

Psalm 92:14 They will still bear fruit in old age, they will stay fresh and green

When I was a teenager in England, I used to go and preach to the old people in an old people's home where my mother worked. I even remember one of my messages about:

Luke 13:34 Jerusalem, Jerusalem, you who kill the prophets and stone those sent to you, how often I have longed to gather your children together, as a hen gathers her chicks under her wings, and you were not willing.

I told the story about the farmer whose farm was destroyed by fire. Afterwards he was inspecting the damage and kicked a smoking pile on the ground. Out of the pile ran 6 or 7 little chicks. The mother hen had hidden them under her wings and as the fire swept over her they had been protected but she died. It is a beautiful picture of how Jesus died to save us from the fires of hell.

Recently in Germany I was asked to go and sing in an old people's home. I sang and preached in a room where there were maybe 10 people. Afterwards I found out that the whole thing could be heard in every room over the broadcasting system. On this day, a member of our church who was 108 years old and the oldest person in Baden Wuerttemberg, Germany, was very weak and dying. I went to visit her and I sang her 2 songs: "Amazing grace" and "How great thou art" in German. She was obviously touched. It was a privilege for me to be able to sing for her. We always sing after people go to be with the Lord. But I got to sing to her before she went to be with Jesus. This sister was a big testimony to all the area.

A TASTE OF HEAVEN

Luke 16:9 And I say unto you, Make to yourselves friends of the mammon of unrighteousness; that, when ye fail, they may receive you into everlasting habitations.

This verse says that we will be welcomed when we get to heaven by people that we helped to get there through our finances or witness. I went to an all-night prayer meeting in another church in Stuttgart one night. During a break I was met by 3 different people who said, "Hi pastor Robert, do you remember me? I was in your group in prison." All 3 had been saved in prison and were going on with the Lord. They were EVEN in an all-night prayer meeting praying for the city. It will be wonderful to meet all those whose lives we touched in heaven. It will also be great to meet those who helped us to find Jesus and who helped us to grow in the Lord. In heaven there is one thing you can't do and that is: you cannot witness to people about Jesus. So let's do it now while we have the chance.

HELP IN TROUBLE

Psalm 46:1 God is our refuge and strength, a very present help in trouble.

How true this psalm is. Whenever we need the Lord, he is just a breath, a prayer away. He is like the superhero Superman who hears a desperate call for help and responds in a flash. I have often experienced this. Once I was driving to Scotland in my new Rover car which had German license plates and was built for the German market. I was on the motorway but there were road works and it was getting dark and it was pouring down with rain. Suddenly, an exhaust pipe lay in my path and I drove over it as there was only one lane of traffic. Bang! One of my rear tyres burst and I pulled over to the side of the road. I was a bit shocked and I realised that I had a problem and did not know how to change a tyre on my new car. I held the steering wheel and cried, "Please help me Jesus!" No sooner had I said this prayer when suddenly a car pulled up behind me. It was a police car and a policeman came to my window. I opened the window and he asked, "Do you speak English?" I said, "Yes, I am English but I live in Germany." Anyway I explained to him what happened and then he said, "Give me the keys and I'll change the wheel for you." I was amazed that a policeman wanted to change my wheel for me in the pouring rain. However, he did, and I did not even have to get out of the car. I was amazed but grateful that the Lord had heard my cry. It was also a blessing that only one tyre had burst. Somebody may ask, "Well why did it happen in the first place?" Well maybe there was a reason or maybe the Lord just wants to keep us relying on Him so he can show us his love.

RESISTING THE DEVIL

James 4:7 Submit yourselves therefore to God. Resist the devil, and he will flee from you.

I was in the middle of writing a book called "Jesus behind bars" about the work of the Jesus Group in Germany. Writing the book became harder and harder and my motivation was running out. I asked people to pray for me. One night, I was suddenly awoken and I saw a face in front of me. I remember that I was not scared at all but I realised that this was a demon trying to scare me or something. I said, "Demon, leave in the name of Jesus!" I remember the face looking highly intelligent but evil just like Jack Nicholson the actor. He answered back, "What do you mean, 'demon'? I am satan!" I just said, "I don't care; you go in the name of Jesus too!" The face disappeared. The Bible says that if we resist the devil, he will flee from us and I experienced just that. I had no fear and we do not have to fear the devil. We just have to beware of him. I Peter 5:8 Be sober, be vigilant; because your adversary the devil, as a roaring lion, walketh about, seeking whom he may devour: I think the devil was not too pleased about the book I was writing. I finished the book and it has blessed many people.

HEALED OF A MYSTERIOUS FEVER

Psalm 5:12 For thou, LORD, wilt bless the righteous; with favour wilt thou compass him as with a shield.

Shortly after the previous incident where the devil appeared to me, I was in Munich on business. When I came back, I started to feel ill and a fever came over me. I don't know what it was or if I had eaten something bad. Anyway, I went to bed early. During the night, the fever got worse but something wonderful happened. I felt God's embrace around me and I moved into a new kind of realm. I cannot describe it but it was a realm of beautiful light and peace. My heavenly Father was wrapping his arms around me and protecting me from the onslaughts of the devil. I felt perfectly safe. I must have fallen asleep. In the morning, I felt perfectly well and refreshed with no sign of fever or illness. Praise Jesus! We need not fear illness. The Lord himself is our physician.

PROTECTION BEFORE BIRTH

Jeremiah 1:5 Before I formed thee in the belly, I knew thee; and before thou camest forth out of the womb I sanctified thee, and I ordained thee a prophet unto the nations.

God tells Jeremiah that He knew Jeremiah even before he was born. The incidents that happen before we are born are important; otherwise we would not be born at all. Just as I want these stories to be read by my three children, my father also used to tell us stories as children. He told us how he twice survived death when fighting against the Japanese in Burma during the Second World War. Once he was patrolling through the jungle and a sniper took a shot at him. The Japanese would climb up trees and wait for soldiers to pass by. His head was just passing a thin tree at the time and he heard the bullet ricochet off the sapling. God had saved his life by the tree. That reminds us of Jesus dying on the tree for our sins.

Then my father became sick with malaria or some other fever virus. He was thus unable to go out on patrol. During this time there was one patrol where a lot of his unit were killed in an ambush. God saved his life again. If my father had been killed in action I would not have been born. The Lord knew me before He formed me in my mother's womb. That is encouraging to know.

My parents

SAVED FROM AN UNSEEN DEATH THREAT

Psalm 91:5 Thou shalt not be afraid for the terror by night; nor for the arrow that flieth by day.

At night there are things which you cannot see but they threaten your life. We need not fear them. I used to work in Vienna in Austria and every two weeks I drove back to Stuttgart. I usually took someone with me from the lift centre in order to save money and also so I could witness to people in my car. It was a long journey of over 6 hours. One evening I was driving back to Vienna on the motorway and I had one passenger. It was dark, my headlights were dipped and I was driving about 70 mph on the outside lane having just passed another car. Suddenly, to my amazement, I saw a car turned upside down on its roof and side-on across my lane with no lights on it. It just loomed into view and I had to react instantly which I did. I instinctively turned sharp right and just managed to swing around the car. Praise God, there were no cars in my close vicinity in the inside lane, otherwise it would have been a fatal manoeuvre. My passenger was shocked and afterwards said, "We are both starting a new life from now on." I stopped shortly afterwards and we informed the police. The Lord had certainly saved our lives that evening. The car must have come from the other side of the road but I never discovered the truth.

HEALED OF SCIATICA

Exodus 15:26 And said, If thou wilt diligently hearken to the voice of the LORD thy God, and wilt do that which is right in his sight, and wilt give ear to his commandments, and keep all his statutes, I will put none of these diseases upon thee, which I have brought upon the Egyptians: for I am the LORD that healeth thee.

A year ago I started to feel pain in my thighs and back and suddenly I couldn't sit down for long and I couldn't sleep. The problem was that there was no position in which I could lie without being in pain. I think not being able to sleep is the worst thing that can happen. I realised that I had a problem with my sciatic nerve. I had heard about others who had had this and knew that it can last for ages. So I prayed, "Lord, I don't think it is Your will for me not being able to sleep so please heal me." After this prayer, the pain started to leave and I had a beautiful night's sleep. In 1984 I committed my body to the Lord and asked the Lord to be my doctor and keep me healthy. The Lord has been good and I continue to trust him.

JESUS PROVIDES ME WITH A CAR

Proverbs 28:27 Those who give to the poor will lack nothing, but those who close their eyes to them receive many curses.

At the end of 2009, my Audi was due for the German MOT and failed. It would have cost me a lot of money to get it repaired and anyway I would not be allowed to drive this car in Germany after July 2020 due to the environmental laws. So I was stuck with the problem of having no car and I was out of work so I had no money either. I got up the next morning and said to the Lord, "Lord, please help me to get a car today. I don't have any money but that is no problem for You." After this prayer I started to think about what I could do. A few months before, my ex-wife had promised to give me some money back because I had been faithfully paying to support the children so I rang her and asked how much she wanted to give me. She said that she would give me €1500. I then thought of a brother in my church who had repaired my last car for me so I rang him and asked him if he had an idea where I could get a car. He said that he happened to have a car there and that I should come over. I travelled to his house and he showed me a Citroen that was in immaculate condition and was 2 years younger than my car and was allowed to be driven in Germany without restriction. It also had very low mileage. He said that I could have it for (guess what) €1500!!!!! So the Lord had provided me with a car that day and I did not pay a cent of my own money for it. The insurance and tax were also a lot cheaper than my previous car.

HEALED OF DIABETES

John 6:11-12 And Jesus took the loaves; and when he had given thanks, he distributed to the disciples, and the disciples to them that were set down; and likewise of the fishes as much as they would. When they were filled, he said unto his disciples, Gather up the fragments that remain, that nothing be lost.

It says in this Bible passage that when Jesus fed the multitudes with five loaves and two fishes that the people could eat as much as they wanted until they were full. Jesus is not stingy when He gives us things. The problem is that we are sometimes not hungry enough to receive all that He has for us. I am hungry for everything He has to give us. Some Christians are satisfied with little.

Matthew 15:26-28 But he answered and said, It is not meet to take the children's bread, and to cast it to dogs. And she said, Truth, Lord: yet the dogs eat of the crumbs which fall from their masters' table. Then Jesus answered and said unto her, O woman, great is thy faith: be it unto thee even as thou wilt. And her daughter was made whole from that very hour.

In this passage we see that the children's bread includes healing and deliverance. In this case it was the healing of the woman's daughter.

One of my biggest tests came in 2010 when I woke up one morning and both legs were numb from the knee down. The night before, I had also noticed that my left big toe had turned black. I emailed my smallgroup to pray for me. I thought there was a problem with my circulation. The verse for the day was:

> *John 10:10 The thief cometh not, but for to steal, and to kill, and to destroy: I am come that they might have life, and that they might have it more abundantly.*

The Lord was showing me that the devil was attacking me but I would survive and experience his abundant life. I do not go to doctors because Jesus is my doctor. King Asa in the Bible had a problem with his feet but he died after two years trusting the doctors and not the Lord.

> *2 Chronicles 16:12-13 And Asa in the thirty and ninth year of his reign was diseased in his feet, until his disease was exceeding great: yet in his disease he sought not to the LORD, but to the physicians. And Asa slept with his fathers, and died in the one and fortieth year of his reign.*

I also asked the pastors to pray with me. My smallgroup leader asked me if she could just check me over and get my blood tested. She phoned me later to say that my blood glucose was dangerously high and that I had diabetes 2. The level was 300% too high! This was a shock but I told her that I was going to trust the Lord and not medicine or insulin. She agreed and gave me some dietary tips. We decided to check the glucose level every day to see the progress. On Sunday in my church in Stuttgart three different people spoke out prophecies from the Lord that were all directed at me. To sum up, they said that the Lord knows my sickness but I am not to be afraid because he will raise me up and make me a blessing for many people.

This was an amazing comfort for me. None of these three people knew what I was going through. I went forward for more prayer at the end of the service. Within days and only one week after the diagnosis, my blood glucose was normal and stable. The numbness in my legs left and I did not have to go to the toilet so often or get up in the night. Also, even though I was eating well, I lost weight and had to buy new clothes. I praise God that he healed me and saved me from a lifetime of injecting insulin and all the symptoms connected with diabetes including the big black toe which is now normal. The Lord also taught me that exercise and a good diet are essential for a healthy life.

After I had told my testimony about being healed of diabetes at my church, a sister came to me for prayer for the healing of her diabetes. Some months later, she came to me and said that her doctor had confirmed that she was healed and took her off all medication. We are blessed in order to be a blessing to others.

THE "JUST IN TIME" JOB

> *Psalm 90:17 May the favour of the Lord our God rest on us; establish the work of our hands for us— yes, establish the work of our hands.*

Since May 2009 I had been searching for a job. In the meantime I was busy serving the Lord where I could in the church and in different evangelistic organisations. I won't list everything but it was a tremendous time. But all the time I needed to find a job to meet my financial needs and responsibilities. It was not easy but I knew the Lord would be faithful.

Recently I went for an interview at a bank. It was funny because I had to go to the interview in a suit which was two sizes too big for me so I had a safety pin at the back of the trousers to help to make them fit me. I lost over 20 kilograms last year after being healed of diabetes. The interview was 2 hours long but it went quite well but they had other people to interview. A lot of people were praying. After the interview I took a step of faith and ordered my "criminal record" in internet which is a requirement if you work in a bank. (Don't worry! I don't have a criminal record!) Today I got the news that I have got the job and will start in the next 2 weeks. This is a big miracle and comes just at the right time because my unemployment money finishes this month. Thanks for all the prayer support and praise the Lord for a miracle. Without it I would have had to leave Switzerland next month. So obviously the Lord wants me to stay in Switzerland at the moment.

> *Joshua 5:12 And the manna ceased on the morrow after they had eaten of the old corn of the land; neither had the children of Israel manna anymore; but they did eat of the fruit of the land of Canaan that year.*

THE JOB WITHOUT AN INTERVIEW

Habakkuk 2:3 For the vision is yet for an appointed time, but at the end it shall speak, and not lie: though it tarry, wait for it; because it will surely come, it will not tarry.

After working 5 months at a bank they decided to stop my project and I lost my job at the end of August. Interestingly, I received an email at the beginning of September that they needed to translate a book of my Pastor's into English quickly so it could be published in English. I also received a request from a friend to translate all the testimonies and additional text in a sports Bible into English which will be given away free to all the athletes in the 2012 Olympics in London. If I had been working, I wouldn't have had time to do all of this but I was able to do it (without being paid of course). As someone said, "If you don't get your miracle then be a miracle!" I was also able to help with other projects during this time such as spending a week in Mozambique helping missionary friends. All the time I tried to find a new job but I found nothing. A brother in my small group had a word for me on 23.9.2011:

"Just wanted to say, I feel you can really just lean on God for your situation. He will provide exactly what is right for you at exactly the right time. It is in his hands just like the 23rd Psalm reminds us. Like a nut that just falls from a tree at our feet when it is just ripe enough, and we do not do anything for it, that's how God will provide for you, at just the right time it will just drop from the tree in front of your feet so to speak. I literally saw this happen before my eyes as I was praying for you this morning. Just keep ploughing away for God. Bless you and be encouraged."

In October I heard that the project where I was before was starting again in January and that they needed a solution architect. I was surprised that I had not been contacted directly but I applied for the job. I heard nothing and when I wrote to the manager, I had no reply. I even saw that the job was advertised in other places in internet. It was very frustrating. I was running out of money and I had to think about leaving Switzerland. I decided to make a step of faith and I ordered and paid for my criminal record which you have to present if you start a new job at the bank.

The next morning I was woken up by a phone call that the bank was extremely interested in me and that I had the job. I did not even need an interview and they offered me more money than when I was there before. So the job came just in time. And the icing on the cake is a rainbow I saw this morning over where I live reminding me that Jesus is with me. (see photo) Praise Jesus.

A LUMP DISAPPEARS

Mark 11:22-23 And Jesus answering saith unto them, Have faith in God. For verily I say unto you, That whosoever shall say unto this mountain, Be thou removed, and be thou cast into the sea; and shall not doubt in his heart, but shall believe that those things which he saith shall come to pass; he shall have whatsoever he saith.

My pastor preached a tremendous message where he said that we should not talk ABOUT our problems but rather speak TO our problems and tell them to go. Around this time, a lump developed on my body which caused me some concern. I prayed about it often and commanded it to go in the name of Jesus. Praise Jesus a few days later, I realised that it had disappeared.

One of the most important principles I learned about praying is contained in the scripture above. Jesus did not say that if you believe, it will come to pass but he said, if you DO NOT DOUBT in your heart AND BELIEVE, you will have what you say. So, when you pray or say, then do not allow doubt to come into your heart and mind for a second. Shut out any thoughts which want you to doubt the Word and promises of God. Doubt can blot out faith. Be like the man in

Mark 9:24 And straightway the father of the child cried out, and said with tears, Lord, I believe; help thou mine unbelief.

After I got this revelation and started to practice it, I started to see even more miracles in my life.

HE GIVES US THE DESIRES OF OUR HEARTS

Ps 37,4 Delight yourself also in the LORD; and he shall give you the desires of your heart.

I never cease to rejoice at how the Lord loves us and is interested in every detail of our lives. I went into a shop to buy some eau de cologne last week and wanted to buy some Hugo Boss but I have to look for a new job again after June so I thought I should use my money wisely and not spend a lot of money on eau de cologne. I decided instead to buy 3 of the Hello Future books at ICF and give them to people I wanted to encourage. On Monday I went to work and a colleague, who had been on holiday in Turkey, gave me a gift which he had bought at the duty free shop -- a bottle of Hugo Boss eau de cologne!!! Wow! The Lord will also provide me with a new job or show me what He wants to do with me next.

FIRED BUT THEN HIRED

Isaiah 54:17 no weapon forged against you will prevail, and you will refute every tongue that accuses you. This is the heritage of the servants of the Lord, and this is their vindication from me,' declares the Lord.

In my last testimony I wrote: "Wow! The Lord will also provide me with a new job or show me what He wants to do with me next." This was because I was given notice at work (I was fired) to the end of June when my contract runs out at the bank where I work. My department had no

budget more so they had to get rid of people. I prayed about the situation and in the ICF international prayer meeting we had a special night when we prayed for people who needed jobs or better jobs. Leo also preached about being a Christian at work and also prayed for people to get jobs. The next day Monday I got a phone call early in the morning saying that the bank had reversed my notice and needed me for a new project!!!! So praise the Lord who can turn any situation around in order to bless us.

JESUS PAYS MY TAXES

Matthew 17:24-27 And when they were come to Capernaum, they that received tribute money came to Peter, and said, Doth not your master pay tribute? He saith, Yes. And when he was come into the house, Jesus prevented him, saying, What thinkest thou, Simon? of whom do the kings of the earth take custom or tribute? of their own children, or of strangers? Peter saith unto him, Of strangers. Jesus saith unto him, Then are the children free. Notwithstanding, lest we should offend them, go thou to the sea, and cast an hook, and take up the fish that first cometh up; and when thou hast opened his mouth, thou shalt find a piece of money: that take, and give unto them for me and thee.

After losing my job in August my money was running out and after 4 months, I had nothing to live on but the Lord always provided in many ways. One day I was shocked to get a tax bill from the tax authorities for 2008. I pay source taxes but through a mistake of my employer I owed the tax office money. However, I did not have the money to pay this big bill. Over Christmas I decided to do the opposite of what you would expect if someone has no money and so I made food packets and gifts to bring to homeless people on the streets at Christmas. I also put a New Testament in with the packets and told the people I met, that this packet was from Jesus. Later I was reading Matthew's Gospel and came across chapter 17 where Jesus paid his and Peter's temple tax by Peter catching a fish with a coin in its mouth. I said, "Jesus, you paid Peter's taxes and I thank you that you will pay mine too." When I got back home in Zürich after Christmas, I found a letter from the tax authorities. It was my tax bill for 2009 and this time, instead of me owing a lot of money, they owed ME a lot of money which paid my tax debt for 2008 and left enough to survive on in January until my first pay came in in February from my new job. Praise Jesus.

MY GUITAR PROTECTED FROM DAMAGE

Daniel 3:26 And the princes, governors, and captains, and the king' counsellors, being gathered together, saw these men, upon whose bodies the fire had no power, nor was an hair of their head singed, neither were their coats changed, nor the smell of fire had passed on them.

As I was packing my stuff to travel to Germany I was in stress and packed my car and closed the garage door and drove away but noticed that something was wrong. I stopped the car and looked underneath and to my horror realised that I had forgotten to pack my guitar and had driven over it and it was continuing to be dragged under the car. See the photo I enclose and you will see that the case was completely ripped and destroyed. But then, when I examined the guitar, there was not a scratch on it and it played perfectly - praise the Lord!!!! On the retreat I was then able to bless people with my music.

The damaged guitar case

WONDERS AT WORK

Daniel 5:12 He did this because Daniel, whom the king called Belteshazzar, was found to have a keen mind and knowledge and understanding, and also the ability to interpret dreams, explain riddles and solve difficult problems. Call for Daniel, and he will tell you what the writing means.'

In my new job at the bank we have a prayer meeting and we were recently reading the above passage in Daniel.

After this I experienced this in my own life. I do not think I am super clever or intelligent but when I have a task to do, I always pray to the Lord for help. On two occasions some colleagues had some programming tasks using DB2 and SQL which no one could solve. These are all colleagues with a lot of experience. I have only been in the bank a few weeks but they asked me for help. I prayed and in both case the Lord showed me how to program the solutions and they worked amazingly well. The colleagues were absolutely amazed. They all know that I am a Christian so the Lord gets the glory.

IT JUST KEEPS ON PRINTING

I Kings 17:12-15 And she said, As the LORD thy God liveth, I have not a cake, but an handful of meal in a barrel, and a little oil in a cruse: and, behold, I am gathering two sticks, that I may go in and dress it for me and my son, that we may eat it, and die.

And Elijah said unto her, Fear not; go and do as thou hast said: but make me thereof a little cake first, and bring it unto me, and after make for thee and for thy son.

For thus saith the LORD God of Israel, The barrel of meal shall not waste, neither shall the cruse of oil fail, until the day that the LORD sendeth rain upon the earth.

And she went and did according to the saying of Elijah: and she, and he, and her house, did eat many days.

I lost my job one August and for 5 months I had no income. I experienced the Lord's help in many ways. I use my printer a lot for the Lord, printing CDs and DVDs which I give away as well as song lyrics and things for the church. Printer cartridges are awfully expensive and my cartridges were both showing that they were empty already in August. However, we have January already and my printer is still printing as well as ever nearly 6 months later. I have never had a cartridge as long as this and shortly after the message comes that they are empty, the quality of print begins to fade. This has to be a miracle.

We are now at the beginning of February and my first pay has come in from my new job and, guess what, the ink cartridge is running out. Just like the widow here it says:

> *The barrel of meal shall not waste, neither shall the cruse of oil fail, until the day that the LORD sendeth rain upon the earth.*

A GIRL DECIDES AGAINST ABORTION

Ps. 127:3 Lo, children are a heritage of the LORD: and the fruit of the womb is his reward.

I was inspired one day to write a song against abortion. It is an issue I feel very strongly about and I thought that maybe a song could be used to help people faced with the decision whether to have an abortion or not, to decide against it. I recorded myself singing the song and I put it in YouTube and Godtube where it has been seen several thousand times.

One day I received an email from a girl in the USA saying that she was moved by the song and had a friend who was going to have an abortion that week. I told her that I would pray and also ask our prayer team at church to pray for a miracle that the girl would change her mind. I informed the prayer team and we prayed. A few days later I heard that the girl had heard my song and changed her mind and she also wrote thanking us for our prayers. If only one baby's live was saved then it was worth writing the song.

MOMMY

Mommy, I'd like to be a pop star;
I want you to be proud of me;
But now it seems my life is over;
I guess it wasn't meant to be.
Mommy I'm not feeling alright.
It's not the way I like to feel.
I need your love to hold me so tight;
To let me know that it's not real.

Chorus
Oh mommy I just want to tell you
How much you really mean to me
If there's just still some way to save me,
We'd be together eternally.

Mommy I wouldn't cry too often.
Just when I want to feel you near.
But now I'm sad it's soon all over.
Oh mommy won't you dry my tears.

Mommy if you could only see me.
My blue eyes and my tiny hands.
If you could see me take my first step;
I'm sure that you would change your mind.

So mommy I guess it's goodbye.
I'll soon be gone from your warm womb;
But Jesus I know will forgive you,
Cus I'll be sure to ask Him soon.

IT'S TIME FOR AFRICA

Jeremiah 1:17 Thou therefore gird up thy loins, and arise, and speak unto them all that I command thee

I wept as I saw the reports of the famine in Africa last year. I knew that I had to do my part in bringing hope to the people.

Someone came to me and told me they had an impression that I would be going to Africa. I kept hearing Shakira's song in the radio "IT'S TIME FOR AFRICA".

At a church prayer night a sister had a word for me, "You will get your visa!" I did not tell people that I understood this message. I had been looking at flights to Africa in Internet and wondered, "Would I be able to get a visa?" The sister's name means "hope" and some missionary friends of mine in Mozambique worked in a ministry with that name. However, I was out of work and had no money so I told the Lord that I would fly to Mozambique if he gave me a ticket. I was asked to help with the prayer ministry at the evening service and as I was waiting to do it someone gave me an envelope and in it was 1000 CHF which was exactly the price of the flight to Mozambique. So I flew there and the trip was a blessing, but that is another story. I got my visa by the way.

ONE STAR HOTEL CHRISTMAS MUSICAL

Exodus 15:2 The Lord is my strength and song, and he is become my salvation...

Sometimes things do not always work out as one expects. One day my car broke down. This meant that I had to travel by train to Stuttgart. However, travelling by train gives you time to read or write. On this one occasion I started to think about an idea I had for a Christmas song called ONE STAR HOTEL. I was really inspired and the whole song came together on the train. When I got home, I came up with a beautiful melody and a song was born. I then had the idea to make this into a whole musical and so I started thinking of a story line and some more ideas for songs. I told a friend of mine David Hardwick that I was working on a new Christmas musical and surprisingly, he asked me if he could help and asked me what kind of songs I needed. I told him I needed songs for the wise men and the shepherds and the flight from Bethlehem to Egypt. He wrote some amazing songs and also got inspired to write a lullaby which Mary sings for Jesus called ONE DAY which is a really moving song.

ONE STAR HOTEL

A cold wind was blowing and the night was falling fast
As the young couple looked down upon the town
The little town was sleeping, Bethlehem its name.
They had reached their destination at last.

They wandered from house to house but every door was closed.
No room for Him who made all things was found.
Just a starlit place with a manger and some straw
Was the last resort that Mary and Joseph chose.

Chorus
Just a one star hotel was all that was found
For the Son of God who made all that we see.
Just a one star hotel, not a palace up on high
Which he left to save the likes of you and me.

Bridge
So there he was born, and the angels watched in awe
As the Lord of heaven took on our earthly form.
In this lowly place came God's mercy and his grace,
His Son who died to save the human race.

And now nothing has changed and there still is no room.
For Him who knocks on your heart's door today.
Won't you open your heart for he longs to come in.
Open up your heart for Jesus who's coming soon.

ONE STAR HOTEL CD cover drawn by me in 5 minutes

FOOD BILL PAID

Luke 6:38 Give, and it shall be given unto you; good measure, pressed down, and shaken together, and running over, shall men give into your bosom. For with the same measure that ye mete withal it shall be measured to you again.

One Sunday I was performing part of my Christmas musical ONE STAR HOTEL which I wrote along with a friend of mine. I also decided to pay for and prepare the food for the meal we had together at church for about 100 people. I was out of work at the time and did not have the money but I was not concerned. On the Friday I was at the prayer meeting and there was a visiting couple there from the United States. After the prayer meeting the husband came to me and heard that I was responsible for the programme on Sunday and said he'd like to contribute towards the food. He placed a banknote in my hand and I thought it was probably a 20 franc note or something. When I later looked at the note, I was surprised to see it was a 200 franc note. The food bill came to exactly 200 francs.

"SOMETHING GREAT WILL HAPPEN"

Jeremiah 33:3 Call unto me, and I will answer thee, and show thee great and mighty things, which thou knowest not.

I was out of work and was working as a volunteer in an organisation in Switzerland which did street work and helped drug addicts and homeless people. When I got up in the morning, the Lord seemed to tell me, "Something great is going to happen today." I was excited to find out what that meant and I thought that maybe I would preach on the streets and many would get saved or something like that. The organisation also provided lunch for needy people. We started the day with a time of prayer and then each one was given a task to do, like going on the streets talking to people or worshipping on the streets. However, on this day I was told to clean the kitchen! This was definitely not my idea of doing something great for the Lord but I did what I was told and I and another brother spent that day and the next day cleaning the kitchen from top to bottom. We dismantled everything and cleaned every nook and cranny. What happened a few days later really blew my mind. The health inspectors made a surprise visit and on inspecting the kitchen they found everything perfectly OK. If they had come the week before, they might have closed the organisation down. So the Lord really did do something great that day!

HEALED OF BELL'S PALSY

Psalm 43:5 Why art thou cast down, O my soul? and why art thou disquieted within me? hope in God: for I shall yet praise him, who is the health of my countenance, and my God.

I was in Israel for several days to attend the wedding of a friend near Tel Aviv but I also visited Jerusalem for a day on the Feast of Tabernacles. For the second time in my life I visited the Wailing Wall in order to place a written prayer in the wall. I wrote down my prayer on a piece of paper and walked up to the wall when a rabbi said to me, "May your prayers be answered." I wrote on the piece of paper asking that the Lord would grant peace to Jerusalem and the whole nation of Israel and then I asked that the Lord would increase the gift of healing in my life.

Some time later in December, I was leading the worship in a prayer meeting when I felt my face going numb and I could not speak or sing properly. I thought I was having a stroke and I asked the people in the prayer meeting to pray for me. I also realised that I couldn't whistle because my face and mouth were drooping and I told a brother that I would know that I was healed when I could whistle again. The next few days it got worse and I couldn't eat or drink properly and I realised that this condition was Bell's palsy caused when an infection cause the nerves to swell and damage each other in the nerve canal. My speaking got worse and my face was badly distorted. It was extremely embarrassing but I continued going to work and leading the worship at the prayer meetings. The condition can remain for years if the nerves do not regenerate. A lot of people were praying for me and the Lord showed a sister that I should try to laugh and resist the enemy who was trying to keep me quiet. The Lord told me to write my testimony to the church before the healing happened because "Faith is the evidence of things not seen." Hebrews 11:1 During this time, the Lord also gave me Psalm 43:5 where it says that he is the health of my countenance.

Two weeks after the paralysis came I was supposed to speak and sing at an Christmas Eve dinner for poor and lonely people and I said to the Lord, "Lord, I need my voice to speak and sing and I want to give a testimony of how you healed my face." The healing came and I was able to whistle and I spoke and sang at the dinner and gave my testimony to the 70 people present. On my last day of work I demonstrated to amazed colleagues in a meeting at work that I was healed by saying a well-known tongue twister "Betty bought a bit of butter but the bit of butter Betty bought was bitter etc. etc." The week before I could not do this or even say words beginning with "B".

This experience strengthened my faith and since then many people have been healed after I prayed for them fulfilling my prayer at the Wailing Wall.

FINGER HEALED BEFORE THE PRAYER

1000 CHF a month.

> *Matthew 6:8 KJV*
> *Be not ye therefore like unto them: for your Father knoweth what things ye have need of, before ye ask him.*
>
> *Isaiah 65:24 And it shall come to pass, that before they call, I will answer; and while they are yet speaking, I will hear.*

I had been out of work for some time again. One day, a sister sent me a text asking me to pray for her finger which had had pain and cramps for several days. I read the message maybe an hour later and wrote her a prayer back speaking healing to the finger. She then texted me back saying that something strange happened. She wrote that as soon as she sent the text, the finger was immediately healed and the pain left. So, even before my prayer arrived, her finger got healed. This sounds amazing but if you think about it, with many things we pray about, God has already been working in the past before we prayed in order to answer our prayer. God desires us to pray but he can answer that prayer even before you pray it because he is not limited by time. It sounds strange but our prayers can change past events because God is outside of time. What happened next was

even more amazing. The next day, I got an email from this sister's father. In it, he said that he wanted me to enjoy a better standard of living, so he would transfer 1000 CHF to my account every month till Christmas which was about 6 months away. This made my life a lot easier and I was able to build up my translation work in the meantime.

A PROPHECY COMES TRUE

1 Peter 5:7 KJV
Casting all your care upon him; for he careth for you.

I was out of work again and was in Germany to clear out my flat there and vacate it in order to save money. I did not have Internet at home, so I was in Stuttgart city centre one cold night in December checking my bank account. I was a little bit dismayed to see that there was only €80 on my account. I instinctively looked up to heaven and said, "Lord, what are you going to do now?" Through all my experience with the Lord, I have learned never to worry. As it says in 1 Peter 5 verse 7, we are to cast our cares on the Lord. Let him worry about how he is going to look after you. Where I was standing, there were 6 beggars huddling together on the floor in the cold. I took pity on them and went to a shop at the station and bought sandwiches and drinks for them. They were very thankful. Then, I decided to read my emails before heading home. There was a new email and it was from someone who gave me their phone number and asked me to phone them because they wanted to return something they had taken from me many years ago. I had no idea who it could be. I called the number and it was a lady. I had lent her and her husband some money to buy a flat about 15 years before. They never returned the money and I had forgotten all about it. The lady told me that her husband decided not to return the money because Robert did not need it and he is so naive anyway. She told me that they were now divorced and she was unable to sleep thinking about the money they owed me. She asked me to give her my bank details, so she could transfer the money immediately. She then transferred €2000 to my account. Amazing! Even before my prayer, the Lord had prepared this woman's heart to be the answer to my prayer. I am always amazed how the Lord answers my prayers. What is also amazing is that some time before this, someone gave me a word of prophecy. They said that, "In the night, with giving and receiving, you will get something returned to you." It did indeed happen at night; I did give to those 6 beggars and I did get €2000 returned to me.

THE MATECAT MIRACLE

Acts 2:6-8 KJV
Now when this was noised abroad, the multitude came together, and were confounded, because that every man heard them speak in his own language. And they were all amazed and marvelled, saying one to another, Behold, are not all these which speak Galileans? And how hear we every man in our own tongue, wherein we were born?

Matecat is a computer-aided translation tool which I use to do translations. I was given a large project to translate with about 17000 words and was given 9 days to finish it. I worked very hard but on the Sunday before the delivery on Monday morning, it was 4am and I still had 2400 words left to translate. I wanted to have Sunday free, so I could go to church. I was very tired and desperate and I started to cry a bit. In my desperation I looked up to heaven and said, "Lord, I could really use your help now." Suddenly, I pressed ENTER on my laptop having just translated a sentence and the word count at the bottom of the screen dropped from 2400 to 450. This meant that 1950 words had suddenly been translated. I was astonished and I felt the presence of the Lord in the room. At first, I thought there must be something wrong with the program. I tried refreshing the screen but the count remained the same. I had been using this tool for over a year and nothing like this had ever happened. It was a miracle of God's love for me. It was not a coincidence because it happened after I prayed. I was able to translate the remaining 450 words in 2 hours and I had Sunday free. On Monday, I delivered the work and asked my employer if he could explain what happened. I explained to him what had happened and that I believe in miracles and that God helps me when I need it. He was unable to explain it but he said that the work was so good that he was going to raise my rating. Translators are rated according to the quality of work they produce.

WORKING AS A TRANSLATOR

Deuteronomy 28:12 KJV
The Lord shall open unto thee his good treasure, the heaven to give the rain unto thy land in his season, and to bless all the work of thine hand: and thou shalt lend unto many nations, and thou shalt not borrow.

It had always been an idea of mine to earn some extra money after I retired. I thought of doing translation but it was hard to find enough work and seemed infeasible. However, some translation websites started to appear in Internet where people could submit requests for translations and work would be distributed to translators around the world who worked at home. I submitted my profile to one such site and one day got an assignment to do. They were so happy with my work that they asked if they could send more work. Thus, I was now earning money as a translator and managed to work for 3 online companies. Slowly I improved, and after a year, managed to earn a fair income. All the companies appreciated my work even though I had no formal qualification. My work done translating books for my pastor and others had given me the experience I needed. My church even paid me to translate a new book about Jacob written by the pastor. I even managed to translate this 51000-word book in 2 months which was a miracle in itself.

PENSION HIGHER THAN EXPECTED

Isaiah 46:4 GNB
I am your God and will take care of you until you are old and your hair is grey. I made you and will care for you; I will give you help and rescue you.

Ever since I was a teenager, I have expected Jesus to return any moment. So during my working years and particularly when I was a freelancer, I was never interested in saving into a pension fund. I used to say, "Why do I need to pay for a pension when Jesus will come before I am 65." Well, now I am 66 and Jesus still hasn't come. But I still expect him any day soon. However, I praised the Lord when my pension was double what I expected it to be. It is enough to live on but I like to earn a bit on top through translation work, so I can afford a few luxuries like traveling.

200 CHF RETURNED AFTER GIVING SOMEONE MONEY

Luke 6:38 KJV
Give, and it shall be given unto you; good measure, pressed down, and shaken together, and running over, shall men give into your bosom. For with the same measure that ye mete withal it shall be measured to you again.

A friend, who was not very well off, lost a filling and had to go to the dentist for a new filling. They needed another 200 CHF for the bill, so I gave them 2x 100 CHF notes. I gave out of compassion without hesitation even though I did not have a lot of money. The next day I was having a meal with a friend. During the meal, he pulled out an envelope with my name on it and gave it to me. He said he found it in his home while clearing out things but did not know who it was from. I opened it and in it was a nice card, a book and 2x 100 CHF notes. The envelope was from a mutual friend of ours who had given the envelope to my friend to give to me 3 months before. So, God had already prepared to return my money 3 months before. God is a master 4-dimensional chess player.

2 GIRLS FOUND AFTER DISAPPEARING WHILE GOING TO SCHOOL

Psalm 18:6 KJV
In my distress I called upon the Lord, and cried unto my God: he heard my voice out of his temple, and my cry came before him, even into his ears.

One day, I read in the newspaper that 2 children aged 9 and 12 had gone missing near Zurich on their way to school. If you are a parent like me with 2 daughters and a son, this is very disconcerting. I was moved to pray that the children would be found unharmed. The next day, I read that the children had been found in another part of the city and unharmed. If you hear or read bad news the let the Lord use you to pray about it and see things happen.

MY TRIP TO THE UKRAINE WAR ZONE

Psalm 91:4-5 KJV
He shall cover thee with his feathers, and under his wings shalt thou trust: his truth shall be thy shield and buckler. Thou shalt not be afraid for the terror by night; nor for the arrow that flieth by day.

A leader from an organisation called AVC, which works in countries where Christians are being persecuted, came to speak at my church. I was deeply touched by all his stories and decided that I wanted to help on a project somewhere in the world. The brother prayed for me and asked the Lord to show me what I should do and that the Lord would provide the means to be involved. Later, I was reading some of their literature and I saw a photo of a young Ukrainian boy holding onto his mother with fear, pain and despair in his eyes. It made me cry and I decided that I would join a team traveling to the war zone in the East of the Ukraine where war had been raging since 2014. I rang a pastor who was leading the team and after asking me several questions and informing me that it would be dangerous, he allowed me to join the mission. Another brother at church was interested in joining but he wanted us to buy helmets, bullet-proof vests and steel boots :). He was also politically biased against the Ukraine. I knew that, like David, we had to go with the protection and strength of the Lord if we were going to be successful. Our mission was to bring food and supplies to the people in the war zone. We each brought finances to help to buy all the food and provisions we would take to the war zone. I was out of work at this time. However, just before the trip, someone gave me 800 CHF for the trip which covered my flight and most of my costs.

There were 4 of us on the trip, 3 pastors and I, including the founder of AVC. The other 3 could speak Russian which made it easier. We flew to Kiev, stayed overnight with a pastor's family and then took a train to Sloviansk where we stayed with the main pastor Peter. He is a great man of God who escaped death in 2014 when 4 of his pastors were tortured and killed by Russian-backed separatists. Peter managed to hide when the separatists took over his church building as their base. A BIG MISTAKE! They captured 2 other pastors and tortured them and locked them in a room for the night. In the middle of the night, the pastors heard footsteps and someone unlocked the door. It was a man with a torch who beckoned the pastors to follow him. He took them into the office, unlocked the safe and gave them their passports. He then led them out of the building and then vanished into thin air. They were also both puzzled by the fact that they saw hot coffee and smoking cigarettes but no separatists. They had all disappeared like the mysterious man (or angel). In fact, they later discovered that all the separatists in the whole town had disappeared!

In the previous days the separatists had destroyed 1800 houses in the town. The church now decided that they would help to mend and rebuild all the houses in the town and would get all the other churches involved to also help people in the whole war zone. They held prayer and coordination meetings every day, organised buses, collected clothing, bought food, trained the mission teams and sent out teams nearly every day to the war zone. They set up small groups In every village and preached to the people who came. At one meeting when we were there, one pastor from my group preached to a group of 50 people and at the end they all received Jesus into their lives. The love shown by believers was overwhelming the people. When we brought them food packets, they told us that they would starve to death if we did not come. With every visit, we would pray for the people and share Jesus with them. The church also brought people out of the war zone and found homes for them in safe towns like Sloviansk. I was asked to visit such a family. We brought them food and were told that their son had a high fever. I prayed for him and later we heard that the fever left. The church also had architects and builders who could build a new family house in 2 weeks!

During our trips to the war zone we could often hear explosions in the distance and once we were caught in the middle of a shell attack and saw the smoke and explosions in the distance. There was also danger of sniper fire and mines in the roads which we saw a few times. We also visited a soldier's camp and gave them a 2-hour concert while the soldiers sat on tanks.

On Independence Day, it was feared that Sloviansk would again have a big attack and the atmosphere was filled with fear. I gathered all of us in Peter's house together and said we should pray against the plans of the enemy. We did this and there was no attack on the town. The town was so happy that they had a big celebration party and invited Peter to preach to the crowd. The Lord was faithful in protecting us and giving us a successful trip.

MY TRIP TO NORTH KOREA
2015 - SEEING ANGELS

Matthew 24:14 KJV
And this gospel of the kingdom shall be preached in all the world for a witness unto all nations; and then shall the end come.

A church in Holland was preparing a mission trip to North Korea and I asked the Lord for confirmation that I should join it. A visiting preacher spoke at my church on the subject of David and Goliath. I realised that this was God's confirmation because North Korea was like Goliath, a nation which is strongly against the Lord and his people. It's estimated that there are 40,000 Christians in prison camps in North Korea. Having said this, I want to say that the North Koreans are wonderful people and we were welcomed with open arms, also from government officials and military personnel.

I booked the trip and the Lord also confirmed it by providing all my costs with gifts from family and friends.

We were 130 Christians from 17 nations and the trip was organised through the North Korean department of tourism and they knew we were Christians. We were not allowed to take Bibles but we could take mobile phones and cameras. We spent 3 days in Peking in order to train and prepare for the trip. We also practiced the songs that we as a choir were going to sing in North Korea. There were only certain songs that the government allowed us to sing. The only 2 Christian songs that we were allowed to sing were "Amazing grace" and "I will follow him". There were 2 Korean folk songs and other secular songs like "Edelweiss", "My heart will go on" and "I did it my way".

So, we flew to North Korea and toured the country in 5 buses with 3 guides in each bus. In the buses we were able to sing other Christian songs and also tell stories and testimonies. Our wonderful guides heard all of this. From the buses we would wave and smile at people we passed and they would often wave back. It was our way of blessing the people. Everywhere we went, we would pray for the country and its people. We were not allowed to talk to people. We were only allowed to take photos when the guides allowed it. We had to be careful what we chatted about because there were listening devices everywhere and even in the hotel rooms. We went to the border between North and South Korea (DMZ). There, we sang a Korean song and prayed for peace and reunification of the 2 countries. It now looks like this is happening in 2018 before our next trip there in September. We stayed at a beautiful new hotel in a ski resort. I woke up in the night to go to the toilet and I saw 2 tall angels in the room, dressed in long flowing robes. One accompanied me to the bathroom door. It was comforting to know that we were being protected by angels. We visited Rainbow Valley where we planted one of the trees that people were sponsoring to help the country. The government had assigned the valley for this purpose. We also have a café in the capital Pyongyang. We were also taken to a church in Pyongyang.

It is a beautiful building and there were many North Koreans there which surprised us. They also had Bibles in the church in English and Korean. One pastor preached a really good message in English and a choir sang some beautiful Gospel songs. Our leader Matthias was also allowed to give a short message and read the Bible. We were also allowed to sing a song in front of the church. There is a lot I could share but it was a wonderful trip and we were well treated.

GET A CS JOB DUE TO PROPHECY

Isaiah 54:17 KJV
No weapon that is formed against thee shall prosper; and every tongue that shall rise against thee in judgment thou shalt condemn. This is the heritage of the servants of the Lord, and their righteousness is of me, saith the Lord.

I was looking for a new job. I applied for one good job but got turned down even before I had an interview. My agent informed me that my rating for this company was not particularly good and that was why they turned me down. I looked into this and found that my rating had gone down from 9.6 to 5.6. It seems that someone did not like me and gave me a bad rating. There are 2 columns in the rating document and both columns had the same information, so it looked suspicious. I rang my old boss and he did not know who did it but he said that he thought I was a good worker. However, it was not possible to get this changed.

I was at another church one Sunday morning and a sister went up to the pulpit and had a prophecy. She said that she saw 2 guns pointing at someone and that an angel came down and pushed the guns away. She said that this means that someone was being threatened by false criticism but God would stop it and the person does not have to worry or do anything. I instantly knew that this word was for me and the 2 guns were the 2 columns in the rating document.

Soon afterwards, another job came up and surprisingly, they wanted a telephone interview with me. The manager interviewing me said he thought that I was the right person for the job, so he was giving the job to me. His name was - Gabriel (The Archangel)!!! Sometime later, I gave a testimony at the church where I got the prophecy.

Something else happened. I started the job and there were other people starting on the same day. One was a guy called Yomi from London and he instantly realised that I was a Christian. He told me that he had prayed that he would meet a Christian in the company. We ended up being really good friends and would meet nearly every day to share and pray together. He was a young believer and soon got baptised and married. His wife got saved also. He had some health issues like asthma and God healed him at a healing meeting at church. People at work noticed that he seemed healthier and we had opportunities to witness to colleagues.

THE BROKEN FINGER

Job 13:15-16 KJV
Though he slay me, yet will I trust in him: but I will maintain mine own ways before him. He also shall be my salvation: for a hypocrite shall not come before him.

At the age of 15, the ring finger of my left hand got broken during a game at a children's camp. I never had any problem with it until one day when I tried to lift a bag in the house where I was staying and it was heavier than I thought it was and I felt my finger break. I could feel the internal bleeding and I could not touch anything with the finger without feeling pain like an electric shock. The biggest problem for me was that I could no longer play the guitar and the children's camp was starting in 2 weeks and I needed to play the guitar all week there. I have a 12-string guitar and you really need to press on the strings hard to play it. However, my finger was broken and I couldn't even touch anything without experiencing excruciating pain. Obviously, I prayed over the finger but nothing happened immediately. I also knew that this was a test to see if I really trusted the Lord in a critical situation. I was in the prayer team praying for the sick, so was I going to trust the Lord myself in critical situations.

A few weeks later, I travelled to the camp and took my guitar with me. I told no one about my finger being broken. On the day when the children arrived, I went into my tent and took my guitar out of the case, quickly prayed and then tried to play the guitar. It worked. I was able to play my guitar with no pain. I played the guitar all week with no pain. My finger was healed.

TRANSLATION OF A CHILDREN'S BOOK IN 2 WEEKS

John 11:49-51 KJV
And one of them, named Caiaphas, being the high priest that same year, said unto them, Ye know nothing at all, nor consider that it is expedient for us, that one man should die for the people, and that the whole nation perish not. And this spake he not of himself: but being high priest that year, he prophesied that Jesus should die for that nation;

I attended a church in Aarau one day and saw that the pastor's wife had written an allegorical children's book. I picked it up and flicked through the pages and spontaneously said to the pastor's wife, "I could translate this book in 2 weeks for you for free." I was surprised by the words that came out of my mouth. This was the first time I had met her, it was impossible to translate the book in 2 weeks and I needed money. However, she looked incredibly happy and accepted my offer. Being a man of my word, I was now committed to doing this work. So, I received the manuscript from her publisher. I translated the first chapter and the publisher approved it, so I set about translating the whole book. I worked awfully hard and to my surprise, I succeeded in finishing the translation in 2 weeks. Sometime later, I met the pastor's wife again and she told me this story. "Robert, before I met you, I prayed that someone would come and translate my book in 2 weeks for free, so I could give it to a publisher in the USA when I flew there. Then you came along." As the verses from the Bible above show, sometimes God can make people say things which are from him and not from them.

So, without knowing it, the Lord had set me up to become her miracle. If you don't get your miracle yet, then become a miracle for someone else.

HEALINGS USING EMAILS, TEXTS OR SOCIAL MEDIA

Psalm 107:20 He sent his word, and healed them, and delivered them from their destructions.

I have experienced how many get healed through an email prayer or a text. Psalm 107:20 He sent his word and healed them is very fitting to the times we live in where we have the technology to send messages via electronic means. The first time I did this was to a missionary friend in the Philippines with kidney stones. She wrote later, that after she got my email, she had to go to the toilet and all the pain left her. Later the doctors could find no more kidney stones.

Recently, a brother in ICF went into hospital with kidney stones. I was informed, so I wrote him a text prayer and had an impression to tell him to place his mobile phone with the text on his kidney. He felt like a sort of movement in his kidney and the stones disappeared and he was discharged without treatment.

I also sent a text prayer to a sister who was going to her doctor to have her iron level in her blood checked which was exceptionally low. She wrote me later that the doctor wanted to know what she had been taking because her iron level was now normal.

My son lives in Germany and he sent a text to me in Switzerland that he was going into the hospital with pain on his right lower torso and was suspected of having appendicitis. I wrote him a text prayer and told him not to worry because they won't find anything when he gets to the hospital. When he got to the hospital, the pain left and despite all the scans they performed, they found nothing.

Paul, even though he didn't have modern technology, knew the power of written prayers and he wrote many prayers in his letters which still work for us today. For example:

> *1 Thessalonians 5:23 And the very God of peace sanctify you wholly; and I pray God your whole spirit and soul and body be preserved blameless unto the coming of our Lord Jesus Christ.*

When you write a prayer, keep to the following principals:

1. Be **S**hort
2. Be **S**pecific about the problem.
3. Speak to the problem like: I speak to the kidney stones and all pain to leave in the name of Jesus.
4. Quote a Scripture like Isaiah 53:5 By his stripes you are healed.

Now try it for yourself.

I GET A ROOM FOR FREE

2 Kings 4:9-10 KJV

And she said unto her husband, Behold now, I perceive that this is a holy man of God, which passeth by us continually. Let us make a little chamber, I pray thee, on the wall; and let us set for him there a bed, and a table, and a stool, and a candlestick: and it shall be, when he cometh to us, that he shall turn in thither.

I was without a job again and my resources were running out, so I decided to give up my apartment in Switzerland to save money, in the hope of finding something cheaper. The Lord provided me with friends who stored my stuff for free and helped me to clean my apartment and move all my stuff out. But still, I had no new place to live. In the end, a friend said that I was welcome to stay in a spare room they had. A few days later the friend saw an ad on the church notice board saying that a brother in the church wanted to offer a free furnished room to someone who couldn't afford it. I was put in contact with the brother and he welcomed me to take up his offer. He had obeyed God in posting this ad and the Lord provided for me through this brother just when I needed it. Actually, I was able to use the whole house and I lived there free for 1 year until I started to earn money again through translation work which I built up.

THE MIRACLE MAN MUSICAL

Acts 5:14-16 KJV
And believers were the more added to the Lord, multitudes both of men and women. Insomuch that they brought forth the sick into the streets, and laid them on beds and couches, that at the least the shadow of Peter passing by might overshadow some of them. There came also a multitude out of the cities round about unto Jerusalem, bringing sick folks, and them which were vexed with unclean spirits: and they were healed every one.

I had always been extremely impressed by the life of Peter. He was a very impetuous person and often opened his mouth and put his foot in it. However, he experienced some amazing miracles like walking on water or healing people with his shadow. The Bible has many stories of imperfect people who did amazing things like Samson, David and the disciples of Jesus who denied, doubted or deserted him.

So, I decided to write a musical called "The Miracle Man" about the life of the Apostle Peter. Again, my good friend David wanted to help and he wrote 4 beautiful songs including the title song "Miracle Man". I also wrote 4 songs. Maia produced 20 illustrations for the book based on sketches from me. So far, we only have the backing tracks and some demos due to our publisher folding up.

A WOMAN'S FACE CANCER HEALED

Luke 17:12-14 KJV
And as he entered into a certain village, there met him ten men that were lepers, which stood afar off: and they lifted up their voices, and said, Jesus, Master, have mercy on us. And when he saw them, he said unto them, Go shew yourselves unto the priests. And it came to pass, that, as they went, they were cleansed.

One Sunday, a sister came for prayer after the service for healing of face cancer. One half of her face was swollen and she was having treatment. For a young woman to have her face disfigured like this is horrible. I prayed a short prayer speaking to the cancer to leave and for healing and restoration to come to the face in the name of Jesus. I then told her to get checked by the doctors who would find no cancer. Sometimes, I just get bold faith and speak out things like this. I heard nothing more after this from the woman. However, many months later, I was traveling on a bus back to Zurich from Stuttgart and this woman was also on the bus and her face seemed normal. She had changed churches. She then told me what happened. She went for a check-up from the doctors. After examining her, they told her that they couldn't explain it but there seemed to be no sign of cancer. They sent her to a specialist and he also could not find any cancer. She was healed and her face was normal again shortly after. Sometimes we pray for people and don't hear the testimony till much later.

This was also the case with a young man I prayed for who had a rare incurable stomach problem. I also told him to get a check-up and the doctors would find nothing wrong with him. I told him to let me know how it went. I heard nothing. But one year later, I was in a prayer meeting and this young man walked up to me asking me if I remembered him. I didn't but it was the same young man I had prayed for. He had gone to the doctors for a check-up as I told him and they found nothing.

41-DAY FAST

Isaiah 58:6-9 KJV
Is not this the fast that I have chosen? To loose the bands of wickedness, to undo the heavy burdens, and to let the oppressed go free, and that ye break every yoke? Is it not to deal thy bread to the hungry, and that thou bring the poor that are cast out to thy house? When thou seest the naked, that thou cover him; and that thou hide not thyself from thine own flesh? Then shall thy light break forth as the morning, and thine health shall spring forth speedily: and thy righteousness shall go before thee; the glory of the Lord shall be thy rereward. Then shalt thou call, and the Lord shall answer; thou shalt cry, and he shall say, Here I am.

One day, I had an impression that I should fast 40 days because the prayer list for all my friends was getting long and I wanted them to experience breakthroughs. I had fasted 3 days and even 7 days before but 40 days seemed an impossible venture. However, the Lord gave me confirmations through messages or through me meeting people who had done this. One thing was clear - to fast for 40 days needs supernatural determination. You cannot do it on your own. So, I decided to fast from 1 January to 10 February 2014. I would eat nothing, not take vitamins and drink only water, a little unsweetened tea and maybe a black coffee now and again. During this time, I was also in Israel for 6 days but I kept to my fast. In Jerusalem, I was able to walk up and down the Mount of Olives to my hotel without any problems. In fact, I had no physical side effects during the whole 41 days; no headaches, no cramps and no dizziness. Yes, 41 days, because at the end, I had no interest in food, so I decided to go one extra day. After 20 days, I was beginning to doubt if it was even possible for anyone to fast that long. I would slap my own face to tell my flesh to forget about eating because my friends were worth me fasting for them. After 41 days, I decided to eat again having lost 20 kg, which I put on again after 3 months. Several people on my prayer list received their miracle and I even found a new job shortly after.

I may do it again one day. I recently did a 10-day fast when I was in Jerusalem and Tel Aviv. I was praying especially for my smallgroup leader's wife with cancer. She is now healed and free of cancer.

1 MILLION BOOKS SOLD

Now to Him who is able to do exceedingly abundantly above all that we ask or think, according to the power that works in us, to Him be glory in the church by Christ Jesus to all generations, forever and ever. Amen. Ephesians 3:20-21

I met a guy at work one day from Nigeria, so I got talking to him and we became friends. One day, I invited him to church and he started to come regularly and got saved and baptised and joined our prayer meeting. However, he was fired from his job. However, the Lord had other plans for him. One evening at the prayer meeting, a sister had an impression that someone had written an important letter and that we should pray about it. It was my Nigerian friend who told us that he had written a children's book in the original native Nigerian language and had written to the Nigerian government about if they thought it would be a good idea to use this book in all the schools to preserve the language. So, we prayed that he would find favour in the eyes of the Nigerian government. What happened is amazing. The Nigerian government wrote back asking him to have 1 million books printed and delivered to every school in the country. Overnight, he became rich and moved to Nigeria. There, he appeared on TV and in the radio and he had a travelling library, lending out books to children in the country. This book you are reading was probably given to you as a gift as I don't sell my books but I was a little jealous of his success, I must admit :).

DOES GOD HEAL ANIMALS?

Several months ago, someone asked me to pray for a rabbit which was not eating. I like animals and I am sure that God loves animals - he created them after all. However, when preparing myself to send a prayer, I had a revelation from the Lord. I knew this but it had never really sunk in. Let's see what the Bible says.

> *Exodus 11:4-7 NKJV*
> *Then Moses said, "Thus says the Lord: 'About midnight I will go out into the midst of Egypt; and all the firstborn in the land of Egypt shall die, from the firstborn of Pharaoh who sits on his throne, even to the firstborn of the female servant who is behind the handmill, and all the firstborn of the animals. Then there shall be a great cry throughout all the land of Egypt, such as was not like it before, nor shall be like it again. But against none of the children of Israel shall a dog move its tongue, against man or beast, that you may know that the Lord does make a difference between the Egyptians and Israel.'*

Have you ever noticed this? God said that he would go through all the Egyptians and the firstborn would die, not only of the people but also the animals. However, he would spare the Israelites and their animals. That means that the blood of the Passover lamb protected the animals too. Therefore, the blood of Jesus can bring healing to our pets. This completely changed my thinking when now praying for animals. I sent a voice message with a prayer in it and told the person to play it to the rabbit. They did this and told me that the rabbit listened with interest. To be honest, the healing of the first rabbit I prayed for was a bit of a battle. It had other complications and had to visit a vet but eventually, healing came and the owner sent me a film of the rabbit eating with his companion. In Switzerland you always have to have small animals in pairs. Some time later, its companion was also not eating but this time healing came quicker. I was then asked to pray for a lost cat. After praying, they found the cat stuck up a tree and were able to get it down. Next, I was asked to pray for 2 dogs who had various problems. I actually went to visit them and the owners asked me to anoint them with oil, which I did. The next day, the owners told me that they were both healed.

Just a few day ago, I was asked to pray for a dog in another country that wasn't eating. Again, I sent a voice message and told them to play it to the dog who again listened to it with interest. An hour later, they wrote to me saying that he ate 30 chunks of dog food.

So, the answer is "yes", God heals animals.

HEALED WITHOUT REALISING IT

Hosea 11:3 I taught Ephraim to walk, Taking them by their arms; But they did not know that I healed them.

Once at church, a brother wanted prayer for one of his legs which was shorter than the other one. Me and another brother prayed for him. As usual, I had him sit down while I measured his legs against each other and sure enough, one was longer than the other. Then I spoke healing to the leg that it would grow out to the same length as the other. I tell in another story how this was the first healing I ever saw when I prayed for my wife. After proclaiming the healing, I measured the legs again and saw that they were the same length so asked him to walk around and test it. He walked around but wasn't really sure if anything was different.

Several months later, he contacted me and told me this unbelievable story. He needed a new tailormade sports shirt and was at the shop to be measured. The shop assistant told him that one shoulder was higher than the other and wondered if he could explain it. He told the shop assistant that maybe it was due to an inlay he had in one shoe to compensate for one leg being shorter than the other one. So, he took out the inlay and lo and behold, the shoulders were the same height. He then realised that he had been healed all the time but never realised it. So funny.

ANOTHER SOLUTION

Exodus 15:26 If you diligently heed the voice of the Lord your God and do what is right in His sight, give ear to His commandments and keep all His statutes, I will put none of the diseases on you which I have brought on the Egyptians. For I am the Lord who heals you.

I was on holiday in Egypt with one of my daughters. We decided to buy a trip to Cairo to see the pyramids. It was a 6-hour drive there. We enjoyed the pyramids and got in the bus to drive back to our coastal resort. On the way back, a young man opposite me spoke to me and asked me if I had any Aspirin for his girlfriend who had an awfully bad headache. I said that I didn't have any Aspirin, but I had another solution. He asked me what kind of solution I had, so I told him that I'd like to pray for his girlfriend. He had nothing against it, so I asked his girlfriend for her name and spoke healing to her from this headache in the name of Jesus. I then sat back on my seat. A few minutes later, I spoke to the young man and asked if we should ask someone else for some Aspirin. He shook his head, however, and said that it was not necessary, because the headache had gone away and his girlfriend confirmed it.

MY HEAD BANGS AGAINST A BRICK WALL

Ecclesiastes 8:5 He who keeps his command will experience nothing harmful.

One Sunday, I was in church and was in the lounge area. For some reason which I forgot, I ran towards a doorway and tripped over a wooden board that was lying on the floor. I went flying forward trying to keep on my feet, but I was heading towards a stone wall with no chance of slowing down. It's as if time slowed down and I managed to turn my head to the left, so I wouldn't hit the wall face on but the impact was still hard and I felt my head bang hard against the stone wall. It was not a nice experience. God has taught me not to panic in such situations, but I knew I had to act quickly. I instantly looked around for the pastor and rushed to him and asked him to pray for me. We sat down and he prayed. It worked! I had no pain, no bruise, no lump on the head and no trauma or shock. The Lord is good. I still sometimes think about this experience and see it as a miracle that my head was not injured.

SOMEONE'S BACK HEALED WHEN I ENTERED THE HOUSE

Acts 5:15 so that they brought the sick out into the streets and laid them on beds and couches, that at least the shadow of Peter passing by might fall on some of them.

God uses various ways of healing the sick. For example, people were healed when Peter's shadow touched them. Someone prophesied over me that I would see people healed when I entered the room. Some time later, a sister living in my village told me that her son had bad back pain. I suggested that I could pray for him when I went to her birthday dinner. So, I arrived early for the dinner and asked where her son was and she replied that he was in his room, so I walked towards the room and he suddenly came out saying that his back pain just left. So, I just prayed that it would not return which is always a good idea to do when you pray for the sick.

Then there was another situation when our prayer team met to pray together and before we started, one sister said that she had a headache and also back pain. So, I said we could pray for her after we pray for the church service. During the time of prayer, the Lord told me, "Robert, you don't need to pray for her, just tell her that she is already healed." I was a bit surprised, but I stepped out in faith and told her what the Lord had said. She then checked herself saying that she had no more pain. A week later, she confirmed that she was healed and had had no more pain since that meeting. I love it when the Lord works in ways you aren't expecting.

DAVID HOGAN MEETING REACHED ON TIME SUPERNATURALLY

John 6:20-21 But He said to them, "It is I; do not be afraid." 21 Then they willingly received Him into the boat, and immediately the boat was at the land where they were going.

I was at a meeting with evangelist David Hogan who has raised people from the dead and done amazing things in Mexico. The next day, I and some friends wanted to go to another meeting with David, but we set out over an hour later than the night before. We only just got there on time the night before and now it seemed that we would arrive late and miss the worship time. We really wanted to enjoy the worship time. The traffic was also bad. I remembered the story in John 6 where Jesus came walking on the water to the disciple and when he entered the boat, they were immediately at their destination. John 6:21. I said that we should now pray and claim that we come on time to the worship. We did that and we also had a time of praying in tongues. On the way, we saw a beautiful rainbow right in front of us. Unbelievably, we got to the meeting just in time for the worship!

DO WE PRAY FOR THE SICK?

Mark 16:17-18 And these signs will follow those who believe: In My name they will cast out demons; they will speak with new tongues; they will take up serpents; and if they drink anything deadly, it will by no means hurt them; they will lay hands on the sick, and they will recover.

The simple answer is "No". Jesus told his disciple to

Matthew 10:8 KJV

Heal the sick, cleanse the lepers, raise the dead, cast out devils: freely ye have received, freely give.

He did not tell them to pray, he told them to do it – heal – cleanse - raise. We never read about Jesus or the apostles praying for healing or even when raising the dead. Did Jesus pray for the ten lepers?

Luke 17:13-14 KJV

And they lifted up their voices, and said, Jesus, Master, have mercy on us. And when he saw them, he said unto them, Go shew yourselves unto the priests. And it came to pass, that, as they went, they were cleansed.

No. He did not even touch them. He just told them to go and get a check-up from the priest. He asked them to act their faith. However, with healing,

I like to use the name of Jesus like Peter and John with the lame man at the gate of the temple.

> *Acts 3:4-8 KJV*
> *And Peter, fastening his eyes upon him with John, said, Look on us. And he gave heed unto them, expecting to receive something of them. Then Peter said, Silver and gold have I none; but such as I have, give I thee: In the name of Jesus Christ of Nazareth rise up and walk. And he took him by the right hand and lifted him up: and immediately his feet and ankle bones received strength. And he leaping up stood, and walked, and entered with them into the temple, walking, and leaping, and praising God.*

Peter gave the lame man a command to rise up and walk in the name of Jesus Christ of Nazareth. He told him to act out his faith but also gave him his hand to help him stand up. Peter did not pray for him.

However, some may ask if Jesus didn't pray for Lazarus to be raised from the dead.

> *John 11:41-44 KJV*
> *Then they took away the stone from the place where the dead was laid. And Jesus lifted up his eyes, and said, Father, I thank thee that thou hast heard me. And I knew that thou headrest me always: but because of the people which stand by I said it, that they may believe that thou hast sent me. And when he thus had spoken, he cried with a loud voice, Lazarus, come forth. And he that was dead came forth, bound hand and foot with graveclothes: and his face was bound about with a napkin. Jesus saith unto them, Loose him, and let him go.*

No, Jesus just thanked his Father for always listening to him. Jesus was always praying to his Father. However, he raised Lazarus with a command, "Lazarus, come forth!"

Jesus had to be specific in order not to raise all the dead within the sound of his voice.

However, someone may say "Didn't Peter pray when he raised Dorcas from the dead?"

> *Acts 9:39-41 KJV*
> *Then Peter arose and went with them. When he was come, they brought him into the upper chamber: and all the widows stood by him weeping, and shewing the coats and garments which Dorcas made, while she was with them. But Peter put them all forth, and kneeled down, and prayed; and turning him to the body said, Tabitha, arise. And she opened her eyes: and when she saw Peter, she sat up. And he gave her his hand, and lifted her up, and when he had called the saints and widows, presented her alive.*

Well, yes, he prayed but like Jesus, I believe he was just connecting with the Father for this situation. And then he turned to Tabitha and told her to arise just like Jesus commanded Lazarus to come out of the tomb.

In James 5 we read about the prayer of faith.

> *James 5:14-18 KJV*
> *Is any sick among you? let him call for the elders of the church; and let them pray over him, anointing him with oil in the name of the Lord: And the prayer of faith shall save the sick, and the Lord shall raise him up; and if he have committed sins, they shall be forgiven him. Confess your faults one to another, and pray one for another, that ye may be healed. The effectual fervent prayer of a righteous man availeth much. Elias was a man subject to like passions as we are, and he prayed earnestly that it might not rain: and it rained not on the earth by the space of three years and six*

> months. And he prayed again, and the heaven gave rain, and the earth brought forth her fruit.

Here, the elders of the church pray over a sick person and the prayer of faith saves or heals the sick person. I agree that prayer is mentioned here but what is prayer? Later, the example is given of Elijah praying for it not to rain. So, let's look at this passage:

> 1 Kings 17:1 KJV
> And Elijah the Tishbite, who was of the inhabitants of Gilead, said unto Ahab, As the Lord God of Israel liveth, before whom I stand, there shall not be dew nor rain these years, but according to my word.

This is interesting because we don't read hear that Elijah prayed but that he spoke and proclaimed that it wouldn't rain until he gave the word for it to stop, which is what it means when he says, "but according to my word." So, praying can also be seen as speaking or proclaiming that something will happen. Jesus told us to speak to the mountain to be removed and thrown into the sea. So, we can speak to sickness to leave. A lot of Christians speak about their sicknesses, but we should speak TO them to leave.

The last healing that Jesus performed on earth he performed by just touching the wound.

> Luke 22:50-51 KJV
> And one of them smote the servant of the high priest and cut off his right ear. And Jesus answered and said, Suffer ye thus far. And he touched his ear and healed him.

14000 WORDS TRANSLATED IN ONE EVENING

I Kings 18:45-46 Now it happened in the meantime that the sky became black with clouds and wind, and there was a heavy rain. So Ahab rode away and went to Jezreel. Then the hand of the Lord came upon Elijah; and he girded up his loins and ran ahead of Ahab to the entrance of Jezreel.

I took on a book translation project for a pastor in Stuttgart. It was my biggest project yet, with over 80000 words. After only 2 months, I had finished 80% already which is amazing. However, it was hard work and I did not have much free time. One day, a Friday, I felt led to fast one whole day without food or drink for a friend in England who needed a job and whose sister in law was in a mental institute and needed deliverance from a curse (by the way, he soon got an amazing new job and his sister-in-law came out of the mental institute). On the Saturday, I was working on the book and the Lord put the idea in my head, that it would be possible to finish the last 14000 words of the book in one night. This was impossible. I already had 19 days planned to finish it and on average I could only do about 1400 words a day. How can I do 10 days of work in one night? Anyway, I trusted the Lord and took on the challenge. As I worked, I noticed that my pace was speeding up. Suddenly, I was able to do 1500 words in 1 hour. The Lord helped me to stay awake and concentrate and by 10 a.m. the next day, I was finished! I was amazed, and it seemed like I was dreaming. The Lord saw that it was becoming burdensome and helped me to complete the book in one amazing night. Praise the Lord. I still had to spend 4 more days proofreading the whole book.

This was not the end of the story. About 5 years before this, I had promised to translate a book for a brother who had written a book about his battle with an incurable disease. However, I tried to translate the book, but after 3 months I gave up. I had a guilty conscience because of this as I always try to keep my word. After experiencing this miracle of translation, I decided to sit down and translate his book at last. I dismissed all the work I had done before on it and started from scratch again. After one week, the translation was finished! I informed the brother and he was overjoyed. Then I found out that he had written a second book, so I decided to also translate that. Sometime the Lord performs the same miracle three times. The Jordan was parted by Joshua, by Elijah and also by Elisha. So, in about 10 days, the second book was finished. This was alongside my normal work. Translation means that I first translate the book and then I have to proofread the book comparing it with the German version and check for any grammatical errors.

ATTACKED ON THE STREET IN ZURICH

Exodus 14:13 Fear ye not, stand still, and see the salvation of the Lord

I was with a team of 4 sisters doing outreach in the red-light district in Zurich one night. We made little gift packets to give to the working girls there and we gave out literature in their own languages. We wanted to share the love of God with them and pray for them. Nearly all the girls really appreciated this and let us pray for them, even sometimes revealing their real name to make sure the prayer worked. On this evening, it did work. One girl told us she had had pain in her abdomen for over a year due also to female problems. We prayed for her and the pain left. She was almost in tears for happiness. Another girl had pain in her upper chest for a long time. The same happened and the pain left. She really did have tears in her eyes. Healing often happens quicker on the street than in a church setting. The girls will never forget these encounters and we have sowed the seed of God's love in their hearts.

On this evening, I got separated the sisters as they walked ahead. I passed a group of 4 young men and suddenly, one of them grabbed my left arm and wrapped his right leg around my legs, trying to make me fall over. I thought he was going to break my left arm. He started trying to forcibly take off my watch. He mumbled that he was going to steal it. Amazingly, I remained calm and did not say anything or try to defend myself. We always had people praying for us when we did an outreach. Suddenly, the clasp on my watch was unloosed and the watch was dangling on my wrist. I was praying silently. At this moment he let go and backed off. I walked away slowly and looked back and said to all 4 men, "God bless you." Later, when back home, I looked at my calendar for March at home and the verse for March was

> *Exodus 14:13-14 KJV*
> *And Moses said unto the people, Fear ye not, stand still, and see the salvation of the Lord, which he will shew to you today: for the Egyptians whom ye have seen today, ye shall see them again no more for ever. The Lord shall fight for you, and ye shall hold your peace.*

The Lord had helped me to stand still and hold my peace so I could experience his salvation. Self-defence could have been dangerous. I am thankful for all our people who pray for us when we go out on the streets.

Later in the year, we experienced a time where 30 girls received Jesus into their lives in 5 months, mainly due to a sister joining us who speaks many languages, before the coronavirus arrived and everything was shut down in the red light district. The door was closed.

FOOT NERVE HEALED

Psalm 118:13-14 You pushed me violently, that I might fall, But the Lord helped me. The Lord is my strength and song. And He has become my salvation.

For 16 years I have been a volunteer on a children's camp called the Indian camp in Germany. The camp is especially for children whose father or mother or both are in prison. It is also for children of poor households. The children get a week's free holiday. We had a great camp again as usual. At the start of the camp, all the volunteers meet to set everything up and to organise the camp and to pray. One sister arrived and was limping and had a special bandage on her left foot. I asked what was wrong and she told me that she had earlier had chemotherapy and that the chemicals were now slowly destroying the nerve so she couldn't move her foot and that eventually the whole leg would be paralysed. Without hesitation, I spoke healing to the nerve in the name of Jesus. Some minutes later, we all had to get together for our first meeting and this sister came and sat next to me on a bench. She said, "Look Robert!". She was moving her foot up and down and the full movement had returned. The nerve was alive and working again. Praise Jesus.

I FALL OUT OF BED

Psalm 37:23-24 The steps of a good man are ordered by the Lord: and he delighteth in his way. Though he fall, he shall not be utterly cast down: for the Lord upholdeth him with his hand.

The year before this camp, I returned home after the camp really tired and went to bed. The next morning, I woke up and forgetting that I was no longer in a trailer tent on the camp, I rolled over backwards in bed and fell out of bed. The problem is that my bed is 80 cm high, so I fell very hard and I was in pain all over and couldn't get up, no matter how I tried, due to the pain. I was in a predicament but didn't want to think about what kind of damage had been done. I was also not near my phone, so couldn't ring anyone. I had fallen downstairs a few times previously and in those cases I just prayed, which is what I did now. I spoke healing to my body and that all pain would go away in the name of Jesus. Amazingly, that is what happened. All the pain left and I was able to lift myself up and walk around normally. I had no bruises or pain from this incident. I learned my lesson and have never fallen out of bed since that.

NEEDS MET IN THE TIME OF THE CORONA CRISIS

I Kings 17:4,6,14 And it shall be, that thou shalt drink of the brook; and I have commanded the ravens to feed thee there.

6 And the ravens brought him bread and flesh in the morning, and bread and flesh in the evening; and he drank of the brook.

14 For thus saith the Lord God of Israel, The barrel of meal shall not waste, neither shall the cruse of oil fail, until the day that the Lord sendeth rain upon the earth.

Switzerland was locked down due to the virus in March and my translation work started to get less due to companies not working or wanting to save money. However, like with Elijah above, the Lord provided for me in many ways but not through ravens. For example, the Lord put it on the hearts of a young Christian couple I know to bring me a big bag of food every week, and they refused to accept money for it. Each bag lasted me a whole week.

Next, we read that Elijah was led to go to a widow who he was able to bless with oil and meal which never ran out until the drought was over. I was also used by the Lord to help a young sister boost her career as a graphic designer. One week, I decided to fast for three days and pray for a whole load of people who had big needs. I wrote all the people and needs on some cards over which I prayed for three days. One sister wrote to me, asking me to pray for her to be able to buy a tablet with an electronic pen so she could better work as a graphic designer.

She worked as an au pair and did not have much money. I actually considered helping her myself but I also did not have much money due to the lack of work. However, an amazing thing happened. A brother texted me and told me that he and his wife were praying and his wife got an impression that I needed money for something. I told him about the prayer request I had received and he transferred 1200 Swiss francs to my bank account. The sister was then able to order a great 22 inch tablet and pen and there was still money left over for me. Amazing.

NORTH KOREA TRIP 15-24 SEPTEMBER 2018

Before I went to North Korea, I had an attack from the enemy. The incident occurred when I fell out of bed. See this testimony above.

--oOo--

We were about 50 believers from 11 nations on the trip. Half the people were from Holland and then there were people from other European countries, from Australia, from Singapore, from South America and even from Iceland.

My lost keys and New Testament

One day, someone found my shoehorn on the floor of the bus. I then realised that my jacket pocket was open and my New Testament and even my house keys had fallen out. Both were awfully bad. I did not tell anyone about the New Testament because it was a crime to leave this lying anywhere. I could not find either on the bus, so I thought that they must have fallen out going to a restaurant or a hotel. The driver searched the whole bus after we left it and found nothing. A few people remembered someone holding up some keys in a restaurant asking if they belonged to anyone. However, we were now hours away from this restaurant. One of our guides phoned around but no one knew about any lost keys. So now, I really had to pray about this. I have had things returned before and I believed that the Lord could also let the keys drop in my hands from heaven. I lay in bed with my hand open and asked the Lord to bring the keys right there. I also realised that the enemy was trying to make me worry and take my joy away. He came to the wrong address. I kept my joy and refused to worry about it. All things are possible.

4 days went by and we went to the May Day Mass Games event which was amazing. I had an impression that I was going to witness a miracle this night. In front of the guides we prayed for good weather even though it had rained all day and the weather cleared up in the evening. We were a bit sceptical about the event, but it turned out to be wonderful. When we entered this amazing stadium where 200000 people were already, I sat down in my numbered seat behind a row of North Koreans and some foreigners. I sang Amazing Grace out loud to the surprise of my group members as it was not a "wise" thing to do but I wanted to take advantage of the situation to give glory to God. It was so loud in the stadium that I think only those close to me could hear it. But, as I said, the whole atmosphere in the stadium became one of joy and rejoicing over their reunification as a nation with South Korea and all our scepticism faded until we were crying and rejoicing with the crowds also.

After the show we left just before the music ended and on the way to the bus, I started waving to the crowds coming out who were walking in the opposite direction. Everyone started to wave back smiling with enthusiasm and we all ended up forming a line in front of the bus just waving to the crowds for half an hour. We ended up being one of the last buses to leave. Of course, when we waved, we were blessing these lovely people and showing then the grace and love of our Lord and Saviour Jesus.

I got back in the bus. During the ride, I prayed to the Lord and said that he can't want that I have to go home without my house keys and face all the hassle of getting into my flat etc. I sometimes argue with the Lord like this ☺ I stood up and happened to reach my hand into the shelf above my head and my hand felt something. It was my New Testament!!! I put my hand back and I felt my keys. I quickly took them down and was full of Joy. So full, that I thought I was dreaming and asked people to pinch me. I told everyone that the Lord had brought my keys back. The guide and driver were astonished and it was a witness to them of God's love. I gave some gifts as a thank you to the guide and the driver who helped me find the keys.

THE GUIDES AND DRIVERS

We had 2 buses with 2 guides and on each bus and 1 driver. They were all extremely nice and interesting people. The drivers were exceptionally good despite having to cope with very bumpy uneven roads. They stayed with the buses all the time and spent a lot of time during stops keeping the buses nice and clean outside and inside. They were with us for the whole duration of the trip and stayed in all the hotels we stayed in. They had our passports and visa, so we couldn't disappear somewhere. We w were not allowed to leave our hotels. In the buses, we were allowed to sing, pray and share stories and testimonies over the microphone. The guides of course heard everything. One of the driver s said he liked the singing because it kept him awake and he didn't need so much coffee. He even sang us a song himself once. He had a good voice. The guides spoke exceptionally good English and corrected them a few times which they appreciated. I was always looking for ways to bless people in NK so when we stopped for breaks, I always bought drinks for the drivers and guides on both buses. These are things they won't forget. Giving tips is not accepted in NK; I tried it in a hotel, but it was not accepted. However, at the end we collected money and everyone got €100 (about 1 month's wage) and a pearl necklace (either for them or their partner in the case of men). The pearl represented their value in God's eyes.

Our 2 guides also sang some beautiful Korean songs for us. They also let us pray for them when they became sick and they testified that the prayers had worked.

My highlight was when I went to one guide from the other bus to say goodbye. Before I could say anything, she looked me in the eyes and said, "God bless you!" It nearly blew me over.

THE BUS RIDES

We travelled on the buses many hours a day. The roads in NK are not the best and are very bumpy so the driver cannot drive very fast. This had one advantage that we were better able to wave to the people walking. Not many people have cars, so they walk everywhere to school or work in the fields. The land is very cultivated with a lot of paddy fields for rice. The roads are very pretty in NK because they are lined with flowers - every road. Believers in NK know that we were coming so we would wave and smile to everyone we saw knowing that some of these people were believers. Everyone who saw us waved and smiled back enthusiastically. We saw our waves as a way of blessing people and I'm sure that they felt it. Nowhere in the world do you get such response from people if you wave and smile. Just a look from Jesus when Peter denied him brought him to repentance. Our smile of love can show the love of Jesus. I always tried to look people directly in the eyes and smile to show them that they are individually loved.

THE PEOPLE OF NK

The people of NK are amazing. They are very welcoming to foreigners, very polite, very humble, loyal, hardworking, well-dressed and positive. If you look at how everything has been rebuilt after he total destruction by the war in the 50s, you just have to respect their dedication and zeal. The architecture is also very aesthetic and not so cold as European architecture for example. Outside and inside always looks nice. We were in some really first-class hotels. With much manpower and few machines, they have achieved the impossible. Indeed, they are a people who believe that all things are possible. And the Lord can use this attitude greatly in the future.

TRIPS

We visited many interesting places. We went to see a newly discovered waterfall in the mountains. It was discovered in 2001 and has been now opened to the public after constructing a path up to it. It is 75 metres tall and very loud and impressive. We had some time on our hands and the guides allowed us to have a time of worship and prayer at this amazing place.

Again, when we went to visit the one official church in Pyongyang, the guides told us we can do what we want for an hour, so we had a worship and prayer meeting and the guides sat at the back and listened. It was a Saturday so there was no official service, but the pastors were there, so we also took time to bless them.

We also visited a children's camp which had an amazing number of facilities for children like a boating lake and a large swimming pool with some large water slides. Many of us brought football, volley balls, basket balls and other gifts for the children. There were hundreds of children and we were able to play games with them and also take photos and interact with the kids. The kids loved it.

We again visited the DMZ where we sang Arirang, a Korean folk song. The soldiers remembered us from last time because it caused quite a stir on both sides of the border when this large group of 130 foreigners sang Arirang.

Again, we went to the circus like last time. It was really spectacular. I liked the trapeze artistes and how they used the Arirang song as a background for their performance.

Next year

The Ministry of Travel wants us to come next year with 300 people. They will even charter a train for us for part of the trip, so we can travel overnight to places. We may even fly to the North. The dates have already been set to 4-15 October 2019. We may be allowed to have baptisms in the river in Rainbow valley where our sponsored trees are. Also, we may be having a bar-b-q and a worship time on a beach. Come along if you can.

Both presidents of North and South Korea met in
Pyongyang while we were there
This is what was agreed between the two parties:
Pyongyang Joint Declaration of September 2018
Link: https://www.ncnk.org/node/1633

BELIEVING FOR GREATER THINGS

John 14:12 Verily, verily, I say unto you, He that believeth on me, the works that I do shall he do also; and greater works than these shall he do; because I go unto my Father.

All my life I have sought to help others. Today I was in Zürich and talked to a group of down and outs who were drinking beer. I prayed for one who was in a wheelchair. He said he felt something. We will see what happens, but I long for the day when people walk out of wheelchairs. *WE HAVE TO STEP OUT IN FAITH IN THE PROMISES OF JESUS.*

I was once asked to preach in England and after preaching I had two words of knowledge. I got them through feelings in my body where people had problems. One was a specific tooth problem and the other a stomach problem. I spoke them out and they were both confirmed and the people were healed.

Last year I was in the prayer meeting and I suddenly had an impression from the Lord that there was a woman in the room with a problem with the left hand. A sister said that her left hand would often feel numb and she couldn't lift heavy weights with it. I prayed for her and some time later, she told me that since the prayer her hand was perfectly healthy again and she could carry shopping and everything with the hand.

I also had an impression recently in a prayer meeting that someone had a problem in the right knee. A woman had a problem in her right knee and I also prayed for a man with a left knee problem and both were healed. Never be afraid to speak out what the Lord shows you.

We also prayed in our smallgroup for a girl in New Zealand who was in a coma. The girl woke up out of her coma about the same time as we prayed and was allowed home after 2 days. We need to keep on praying and believing even if we think that it doesn't always work. Before the greater works come the works and before the works comes faith in Jesus. I've made it a habit of mine to pray for every sick person I meet, even if it is quietly without the person knowing.

> *Hebrews 11:6 But without faith it is impossible to please Him: for he that comes to God must believe that He is, and that* **He is a rewarder of them that diligently seek him.**

The Lake of Zürich

Zürich

Psalm 78:1-4 Give ear, O my people, to my law: incline your ears to the words of my mouth. I will open my mouth in a parable: I will utter dark sayings of old: Which we have heard and known, and our fathers have told us. We will not hide them from their children, shewing to the generation to come the praises of the LORD, and his strength, and his wonderful works that he hath done.

www.ingramcontent.com/pod-product-compliance
Lightning Source LLC
Chambersburg PA
CBHW021446070526
44577CB00002B/272